Poverty

Other Books of Related Interest:

Opposing Viewpoints Series

Africa

Welfare

Current Controversies Series

Developing Nations

At Issue Series

World Hunger

"Congress shall make no law . . . abridging the freedom of speech, or of the press."

First Amendment to the U.S. Constitution

The basic foundation of our democracy is the First Amendment guarantee of freedom of expression. The Opposing Viewpoints Series is dedicated to the concept of this basic freedom and the idea that it is more important to practice it than to enshrine it.

Poverty

Viqi Wagner, Book Editor

GREENHAVEN PRESS
A part of Gale, Cengage Learning

Detroit • New York • San Francisco • New Haven, Conn • Waterville, Maine • London

Christine Nasso, *Publisher*
Elizabeth Des Chenes, *Managing Editor*

© 2008 Greenhaven Press, a part of Gale, Cengage Learning.

For more information, contact:
Greenhaven Press
27500 Drake Rd.
Farmington Hills, MI 48331-3535
Or you can visit our Internet site at gale.cengage.com

For product information and technology assistance, contact us at

Gale Customer Support, 1-800-877-4253
For permission to use material from this text or product, submit all requests online at www.cengage.com/permissions

Further permissions questions can be emailed to permissionrequest@cengage.com

Articles in Greenhaven Press anthologies are often edited for length to meet page requirements. In addition, original titles of these works are changed to clearly present the main thesis and to explicitly indicate the author's opinion. Every effort is made to ensure that Greenhaven Press accurately reflects the original intent of the authors. Every effort has been made to trace the owners of copyrighted material.

Cover photograph reproduced by permission of Rokusek Design, Inc.

LIBRARY OF CONGRESS CATALOGING-IN-PUBLICATION DATA

Poverty / Viqi Wagner, book editor.
        p. cm. -- (Opposing viewpoints)
    Includes bibliographical references and index.
    ISBN-13: 978-0-7377-3747-9 (hardcover)
    ISBN-13: 978-0-7377-3748-6 (pbk.)
    1. Poverty--United States--Juvenile literature. 2. Poverty--Juvenile literature. I. Wagner, Viqi, 1953-
    HC110.P6P588 2008
    339.4'60973--dc22
                                                            2008014664

Printed in the United States of America
1 2 3 4 5 6 7 12 11 10 09 08

Contents

Chapter 3: How Can Poverty Be Reduced in the United States?

Chapter 4: How Should Global Poverty Be Addressed?

Why Consider
Opposing Viewpoints?

> *"The only way in which a human being can make some approach to knowing the whole of a subject is by hearing what can be said about it by persons of every variety of opinion and studying all modes in which it can be looked at by every character of mind. No wise man ever acquired his wisdom in any mode but this."*
>
> John Stuart Mill

In our media-intensive culture it is not difficult to find differing opinions. Thousands of newspapers and magazines and dozens of radio and television talk shows resound with differing points of view. The difficulty lies in deciding which opinion to agree with and which "experts" seem the most credible. The more inundated we become with differing opinions and claims, the more essential it is to hone critical reading and thinking skills to evaluate these ideas. Opposing Viewpoints books address this problem directly by presenting stimulating debates that can be used to enhance and teach these skills. The varied opinions contained in each book examine many different aspects of a single issue. While examining these conveniently edited opposing views, readers can develop critical thinking skills such as the ability to compare and contrast authors' credibility, facts, argumentation styles, use of persuasive techniques, and other stylistic tools. In short, the Opposing Viewpoints Series is an ideal way to attain the higher-level thinking and reading skills so essential in a culture of diverse and contradictory opinions.

In addition to providing a tool for critical thinking, Opposing Viewpoints books challenge readers to question their own strongly held opinions and assumptions. Most people form their opinions on the basis of upbringing, peer pressure, and personal, cultural, or professional bias. By reading carefully balanced opposing views, readers must directly confront new ideas as well as the opinions of those with whom they disagree. This is not to simplistically argue that everyone who reads opposing views will—or should—change his or her opinion. Instead, the series enhances readers' understanding of their own views by encouraging confrontation with opposing ideas. Careful examination of others' views can lead to the readers' understanding of the logical inconsistencies in their own opinions, perspective on why they hold an opinion, and the consideration of the possibility that their opinion requires further evaluation.

Evaluating Other Opinions

To ensure that this type of examination occurs, Opposing Viewpoints books present all types of opinions. Prominent spokespeople on different sides of each issue as well as well-known professionals from many disciplines challenge the reader. An additional goal of the series is to provide a forum for other, less known, or even unpopular viewpoints. The opinion of an ordinary person who has had to make the decision to cut off life support from a terminally ill relative, for example, may be just as valuable and provide just as much insight as a medical ethicist's professional opinion. The editors have two additional purposes in including these less known views. One, the editors encourage readers to respect others' opinions—even when not enhanced by professional credibility. It is only by reading or listening to and objectively evaluating others' ideas that one can determine whether they are worthy of consideration. Two, the inclusion of such viewpoints encourages the important critical thinking skill of objectively evaluating an author's credentials and bias. This evaluation will illuminate an author's reasons for taking a particular stance on an issue and will aid in readers' evaluation of the author's ideas.

It is our hope that these books will give readers a deeper understanding of the issues debated and an appreciation of the complexity of even seemingly simple issues when good and honest people disagree. This awareness is particularly important in a democratic society such as ours in which people enter into public debate to determine the common good. Those with whom one disagrees should not be regarded as enemies but rather as people whose views deserve careful examination and may shed light on one's own.

Thomas Jefferson once said that "difference of opinion leads to inquiry, and inquiry to truth." Jefferson, a broadly educated man, argued that "if a nation expects to be ignorant and free . . . it expects what never was and never will be." As individuals and as a nation, it is imperative that we consider the opinions of others and examine them with skill and discernment. The Opposing Viewpoints Series is intended to help readers achieve this goal.

David L. Bender and Bruno Leone,
Founders

Introduction

"*The poor will always be with us—just not on the TV news.*"

—*Neil deMause and Steve Rendall,*
Fairness & Accuracy In Reporting, 2007

In 1968 Democratic presidential candidate Senator Robert F. Kennedy embarked on a two-day, two-hundred-mile tour of rural Kentucky to draw attention to the plight of poor Americans, one of his key campaign issues. He was followed by enormous crowds and the national press corps, whose illuminating stories and images ignited both public outrage and government action to rebuild destitute communities in Appalachia.

In July 2007 former Democratic presidential candidate Senator John Edwards announced a three-day, eight-state, eighteen-hundred-mile tour to call attention to poverty in America, his key campaign issue. Every major daily newspaper and three leading newsmagazines initially responded with articles about poverty, but by the tour's halfway point, coverage dropped to a trickle. According to Peter Dreier, professor of politics at Occidental College in Los Angeles, many of those articles reflected "journalistic cynicism" as well; in particular, a *Newsweek* article tried to show that Edwards would not galvanize antipoverty sentiment because "American voters don't care about the poor, because the media aren't paying attention to the issue, and because poverty isn't as serious a problem as it was in 1968."

What has changed? Is poverty portrayed differently by the media today than it was in 1968? And does the *Newsweek* assessment accurately reflect Americans' attitudes toward the poor?

There is widespread consensus that the news industry *has* changed dramatically in recent years. As newspaper readers and TV viewers increasingly turn to the Internet for information, traditional media outlets are forced to cut budgets and staff and devote more and more space to inexpensive programming that does not require big investments of time and investigative expertise. The public appetite for celebrity, sensationalism, lifestyle stories, and other trivial aspects of popular culture has grown apace. Competition for ratings and advertisers is blamed for the willingness of broadcast news to forgo reasoned discourse and feed the public appetite with an increasing diet of "soft" news and infotainment, characterized by many as style over substance.

Critics claim that this trend adversely affects the quality of media coverage of poverty. Katherine Boo of the New America Foundation argues that media portrayals of poverty are too often stereotypical: Stories are generally either sentimental (a self-sacrificing, heroic poor mom struggles to keep her kids clean and fed) or sensationalist (a journalist, often at the center of the story, ventures into dangerous poverty-stricken places to cover drug addicts, a crime scene, or the mentally ill homeless). Others accuse the media of oversimplifying a complex issue: Poverty is too often reduced to stark dichotomies such as nature versus nurture or the "deserving poor" versus the "undeserving poor."

There is considerable evidence that the trend toward soft news has seriously affected the quantity of media coverage of poverty as well as the quality. In February 2008 journalism professor Caryl Rivers described a study by Thomas Patterson, Bradlee Professor of Government and the Press at Harvard, who found that "news stories lacking public policy content jumped from less than 35 percent of all stories in 1980 to roughly 50 percent of stories appearing in 2001."

The strongest indictment of media coverage of poverty to date comes in a September 2007 study by the media watchdog group Fairness & Accuracy In Reporting (FAIR). The authors tracked the three weeknight network newscasts (*ABC World News Tonight*, *CBS Evening News*, and *NBC Nightly News*) from September 2003 to November 2006, and found a total of only fifty-eight stories even remotely dealing with poverty in more than a passing way over the entire thirty-eight-month period. By comparison, the networks devoted sixty-nine stories to pop star Michael Jackson's legal troubles. Even in 2005, the year of the Katrina disaster, the networks ran forty-four stories on Jackson compared with twenty-two on poverty.

The FAIR study also criticized the networks' representation of the poor. The majority of stories that did deal with poverty quoted elected officials and executives of relief or activist organizations, but not the poor themselves. Alternatively, stories that did interview poor people in the context of economic polarization or low-wage workers' difficulty in finding child care made references to "the changing economy" without scrutinizing government policies that might have indicated "what changes were made or who made them," implying that poverty is bad but nobody's fault. Furthermore, poverty stories tended to feature the elderly and members of the armed forces, which the FAIR study interprets as subtle bias against the unemployed or welfare recipients and their children who are less likely to fit a sympathetic "deserving" image. Finally, the FAIR study cites journalists themselves who told researchers that "the poverty narrative is neither compelling nor good for business, as advertisers aren't fond of negative stories."

Other journalists and media analysts would view the FAIR assessment as unfairly harsh, however. *New York Times* reporter David Brooks, for example, says media coverage of poverty has always been "a story of big blips on a blank background." In the twentieth century, the blips—intense coverage for short periods—occurred during the 1930s Great Depression, the 1960s war on poverty, and the 1980s controversy over welfare abuse. The media is not necessarily ignoring a serious problem, if there is, as Brooks says, "in between the blips, nothing." Panelists at a 2005 discussion at the Center on Poverty, Work, and Opportunity pointed out that intermittent coverage is the case in many issues. A steady diet of poverty stories may keep the issue alive, but people tire of any steady diet; it takes a jolt like Hurricane Katrina in 2005 or a major policy development to create another poverty blip and revive public interest.

As for claims that Americans are truly indifferent to poverty, some political commentators suggest that today's middle class is too distracted by its own economic insecurity to be concerned about the poor, and the wealthy are content with the status quo. Dreier, however, disputes *Newsweek*'s message that Americans do not care about the poor. According to Dreier, the vast majority favor raising the minimum wage. Poll respondents express growing concern about the working poor and belief in a widening gap between rich and poor. And the Pew Research Center for the People & the Press reported in 2007 that 69 percent of Americans (83 percent of Democrats and 47 percent of Republicans) believe government "should provide food and shelter for all." The official overall poverty rate in America (12.3 percent) is lower today than it was in 1968 (12.8 percent), but it has risen significantly since its all-time low of 11.1 percent in 1973, and with a child poverty rate now hovering at 20 percent, poverty is anything but a dead issue.

The authors in *Opposing Viewpoints: Poverty* fill gaps in, and seek to improve on, mass media coverage of poverty as they debate complex issues in the following chapters: Is Poverty a Serious Problem in America? What Causes Poverty in America? How Can Poverty Be Reduced in the United States? and How Should Global Poverty Be Addressed? The shrinking proportion of news broadcasts devoted to poverty cannot obscure its relevance at a time when economic security at all but the highest income levels is shrinking too.

CHAPTER 1

Is Poverty a Serious Problem in America?

Chapter Preface

For decades, poverty in America has been a mostly urban phenomenon. In a sixty-year trend that began when GIs came home from World War II, families, retailers, and jobs steadily moved out of the cities to brand-new suburban developments, where car-based living in spacious single-family homes, big yards, and shopping malls represented the new American Dream. Urban property values fell, tax bases crumbled, and as unemployment and crime rates rose, middle- and upper-class residents moved out.

In March 2008, however, University of Michigan professor of urban planning Christopher B. Leinberger warned that "fundamental changes in American life may turn today's Mc-Mansions into tomorrow's tenements" and the American suburb into "what inner cities became in the 1960s and '70s—slums characterized by poverty, crime, and decay." Leinberger identifies several reasons why suburban poverty is likely to become a serious problem by 2025. The most obvious is the current subprime-mortgage crisis: A high-priced housing boom followed by waves of foreclosures, leaving developments where as many as one in four houses have been abandoned, crime rates have risen 33 percent, and signs of physical and social disorder—vandalism, squatters, neglect—are further reducing demand for suburban property. Second, Leinberger points to broad demographic shifts: By 2025 "the U.S. will contain about as many single-person households as families with children," and few singles of any age want or need big houses on big lots. A third reason for suburban flight is steep hikes in the price of gasoline and energy—life in low-density suburbs usually means lots of driving, and it costs a lot to heat McMansions.

Fourth, urban living is fashionable again. Affluent homeowners now pay a premium for "filled-in" period housing within walking distance of shops, schools, restaurants and entertainment, jobs, convenient public transit, and a lively street scene. Poor renters displaced from gentrified city neighborhoods are migrating to fringe areas and suburbs that are poorly served by public transportation. As the outward spread of poverty and neighborhood decline accelerates, more suburban housing will be converted into rental units or sold at rock-bottom prices to low-income families. The glut of McMansions, often cheaply built and much less durable than urban housing of a century ago, will deteriorate fast. Schooling and safety are likely to improve in gentrified urban areas and worsen in suburbs that suffer budget deficits as tax revenues dwindle. In December 2006, a Brookings Institution study reported statistics that support this glum forecast—in 2005, "the suburban poor outnumbered their central-city counterparts by at least 1 million" and "for the first time [suburbs] contain a majority of the nation's poor population." The authors in this chapter debate the distribution and severity of poverty in the United States and the definition of poverty itself.

"The official poverty rate in 2006 was 12.3 percent, down from 12.6 percent in 2005."

Census Bureau Measures Show the U.S. Poverty Rate Has Decreased

U.S. Census Bureau

Every August the U.S. Census Bureau reports the number of Americans living in poverty, using data collected in its annual Current Population Survey (CPS) and its Annual Social and Economic Supplement (ASEC). By "population," the bureau means all noninstitutionalized civilians, as well as members of the armed forces living in a household with at least one civilian adult. By "poverty," the bureau means an annual income below certain calculated thresholds—for example, less than $10,210 for a single person, less than $20,650 for a family of four—based on formulas devised by economist Mollie Orshansky in the 1960s. Since hitting a twenty-six-year low in 2000, the poverty rate has climbed steadily, but according to the bureau's 2007 report, the overall poverty rate fell in 2006. The following excerpt from that report further defines the number of Americans living in poverty by age, region, race, and other characteristics.

U.S. Census Bureau, "Income, Poverty, and Health Insurance Coverage in the United States: 2006," Washington, DC., U.S. Census Bureau, 2007.

21

As you read, consider the following questions:

1. How many Americans does the U.S. Census Bureau currently define as poor?

2. According to the authors, what is the poverty rate among children in America?

3. According to the Census Bureau, how many Americans live in so-called deep poverty?

This presents data on income, poverty, and health insurance coverage in the United States based on information collected in the 2007 and earlier Annual Social and Economic Supplements (ASEC) to the Current Population Survey (CPS) conducted by the U.S. Census Bureau.

Data presented in this report indicate the following:

• Real median household income increased between 2005 and 2006 for the second consecutive year.

• The poverty rate decreased between 2005 and 2006.

• The number of people with health insurance coverage increased between 2005 and 2006, as did the number and the percentage of people without health insurance coverage.

These results were not uniform across demographic groups. For example, between 2005 and 2006, the median income of White households rose, but it remained statistically unchanged for the remaining race groups and Hispanics; the poverty rate decreased for Hispanics but remained statistically unchanged for non-Hispanic Whites, Blacks, and Asians; and the percentage of people without health insurance increased for Hispanics, decreased for Asians, and remained statistically unchanged for non-Hispanic Whites and Blacks. . . .

The income and poverty estimates shown in this report are based solely on money income before taxes and do not include the value of noncash benefits such as food stamps, Medicare, Medicaid, public housing, and employer-provided fringe benefits. . . .

Poverty in the United States

- The official poverty rate in 2006 was 12.3 percent, down from 12.6 percent in 2005.

- In 2006, 36.5 million people were in poverty, not statistically different from 2005.

- Poverty rates in 2006 were statistically unchanged for non-Hispanic Whites (8.2 percent), Blacks (24.3 percent), and Asians (10.3 percent) from 2005. The poverty rate decreased for Hispanics (20.6 percent in 2006, down from 21.8 percent in 2005).

- The poverty rate in 2006 was lower than in 1959, the first year for which poverty estimates are available. From the most recent trough in 2000, the rate rose for 4 consecutive years, from 11.3 percent in 2000 to 12.7 percent in 2004, and then declined to 12.3 percent in 2006—a rate not statistically different from those in 2002 and 2003 (12.1 percent and 12.5 percent, respectively).

- For children under 18 years old and people aged 18 to 64, the poverty rates (17.4 percent and 10.8 percent, respectively) and the numbers in poverty (12.8 million and 20.2 million, respectively) remained statistically unchanged from 2005.

- Both the poverty rate and the number in poverty decreased for people aged 65 and older (9.4 percent and 3.4 million in 2006, down from 10.1 percent and 3.6 million in 2005).

Race and Hispanic Origin

At 8.2 percent, the 2006 poverty rate for non-Hispanic Whites was lower than the rate for Blacks and Asians, 24.3 percent and 10.3 percent, respectively. For all three of these groups, the number and the percentage in poverty were statistically unchanged between 2005 and 2006. In 2006, non-Hispanic Whites accounted for 43.9 percent of people in poverty and 66.1 percent of the total population. Among Hispanics, 20.6 percent were in poverty in 2006, lower than the 21.8 percent in 2005, while the number of Hispanics in poverty remained statistically unchanged at 9.2 million in 2006.

Age

Both the poverty rate and the number in poverty for people aged 18 to 64 were not statistically different from 2005, at 10.8 percent and 20.2 million in 2006. In contrast, both the poverty rate and the number of people 65 and older in poverty decreased to 9.4 percent and 3.4 million in 2006 from 10.1 percent and 3.6 million in 2005.

In 2006, children under 18 showed no statistical change in their poverty rate or the number in poverty (17.4 percent and 12.8 million). The poverty rate for children was higher than the rates for people 18 to 64 years old and those 65 and older. Children represented 35.2 percent of the people in poverty and 24.9 percent of the total population.

In 2006, the poverty rate for related children under 18 living in families was 16.9 percent, statistically unchanged from 2005. For related children under 18 living in families with a female householder with no husband present, 42.1 percent were in poverty compared with 8.1 percent for married-couple families.

The poverty rate and the number in poverty for related children under 6 living in families were 20.0 percent and 4.8 million, both not statistically different from 2005. Of related children under 6 living in families with a female householder with no husband present, 52.7 percent were in poverty, over five times the rate of their counterparts in married-couple families (9.4 percent).

Nativity

Of all people, 87.4 percent were native born, 4.9 percent were foreign-born naturalized citizens, and 7.7 percent were foreign-born noncitizens. The poverty rate and the number in poverty for the native-born population were not statistically different from 2005 at 11.9 percent and 30.8 million in 2006. The poverty rate for the foreign-born population decreased from 16.5 percent in 2005 to 15.2 percent in 2006, while the number in poverty remained statistically unchanged at 5.7 million in 2006.

Of the foreign-born population, 39.0 percent were naturalized citizens; the remaining were noncitizens. Their poverty rates in 2006 were 9.3 percent for foreign-born naturalized citizens and 19.0 percent for those who were not U.S. citizens, both statistically unchanged from 2005.

Region

In 2006, the South continued to have the highest poverty rate at 13.8 percent. The other three regions had poverty rates that were not statistically different from one another—11.5 percent in the Northeast, 11.2 percent in the Midwest, and 11.6 percent in the West. The West was the only region to show a statistical change in the number and the percentage in poverty— 8.0 million and 11.6 percent in 2006, down from 8.6 million and 12.6 percent in 2005.

The poverty rate and the number of people in poverty in metropolitan statistical areas (principal cities and suburbs) were 11.8 percent and 29.3 million in 2006, down from 12.2 percent and 30.1 million in 2005. Of all people in metropolitan statistical areas in 2006, 38.2 percent lived in principal cities, and 52.4 percent of people in poverty in those metropolitan statistical areas lived in principal cities.

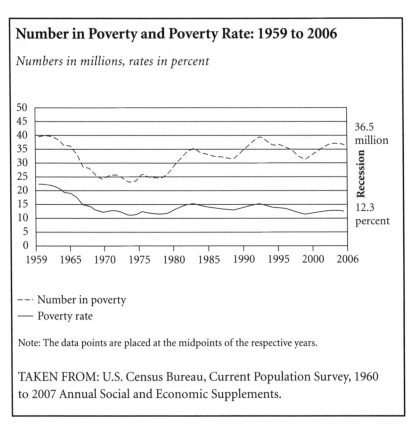

Number in Poverty and Poverty Rate: 1959 to 2006

Numbers in millions, rates in percent

--- Number in poverty
— Poverty rate

Note: The data points are placed at the midpoints of the respective years.

TAKEN FROM: U.S. Census Bureau, Current Population Survey, 1960 to 2007 Annual Social and Economic Supplements.

The poverty rate and the number in poverty decreased for people living inside principal cities, from 17.0 percent and 16.0 million in 2005 to 16.1 percent and 15.3 million in 2006. The poverty rate and the number in poverty for people living in the suburbs were 9.1 percent and 13.9 million in 2006, statistically unchanged from 2005.

Among those living outside metropolitan statistical areas, the poverty rate and the number in poverty were 15.2 percent and 7.2 million in 2006, statistically unchanged from 2005.

Work and Family Status

People 16 and older who worked some or all of 2006 had a lower poverty rate than those who did not work at any time (5.8 percent compared with 21.1 percent). The poverty rate among full-time, year-round workers (2.7 percent) was lower than the rate for those who worked part-time or part-year (12.6 percent) in 2006. In addition, among people 16 and older, those who did not work in 2006 represented 43.1 percent of people in poverty, compared with 25.1 percent of all people.

In 2006, the poverty rate and the number of families in poverty were 9.8 percent and 7.7 million, both statistically unchanged from 2005.

Furthermore, the poverty rate and the number in poverty showed no change between 2005 and 2006 for the different types of families. In 2006, married-couple families (4.9 percent and 2.9 million), female-householder-with-no-husband-present families (28.3 percent and 4.1 million), and male-householder-with-no-wife-present families (13.2 percent and 671,000) were all statistically unchanged from 2005.

Depth of Poverty

Categorizing people as "in poverty" or "not in poverty" is one way to describe their economic situation. The income-to-poverty ratio and the income deficit (surplus) describe other aspects of economic well-being. Where the poverty rate provides a measure of the proportion of people with a family income that is below the established poverty thresholds, the income-to-poverty ratio provides a measure to gauge the depth of poverty and to calculate the size of the population that may be eligible for government-sponsored assistance programs, such as Temporary Assistance for Needy Families (TANF), Medicare, food stamps, and the Low-Income Home Energy Assistance Program (LIHEAP). The income-to-poverty ratio is reported as a percentage that compares a family's or an unrelated individual's (person who does not live with relatives) income with their poverty threshold. For example, a family or individual with an income-to-poverty ratio of 110 percent has income that is 10 percent above their poverty threshold.

The income deficit (surplus) tells how many dollars a family's or an unrelated individual's income is below (above) their poverty threshold. These measures illustrate how the low-income population varies in relation to the poverty thresholds. . . .

In 2006, 5.2 percent, or 15.4 million people, had an income below one-half their poverty threshold. This group represented 42.4 percent of the poverty population in 2006. The percentage and the number of people with income below 125 percent of their threshold was 16.8 percent and 49.7 million. For children under 18 years old, 7.5 percent (5.5 million) were below 50 percent of their poverty thresholds, and 23.1 percent (17.1 million) were below 125 percent of their thresholds.

The demographic makeup of the population differs at varying degrees of poverty. In 2006 among all people, 5.2 percent were below 50 percent of their threshold, 7.1 percent were at or above 50 percent and below 100 percent of their threshold, and 4.5 percent were between 100 percent and 125 percent of their thresholds. The 65-and-older population was more highly concentrated between 100 percent to 125 percent of their poverty thresholds (6.2 percent) than below 50 percent of their thresholds (2.5 percent). Among people 65 and older, 9.4 percent were below 100 percent of poverty, and 15.6 percent were below 125 percent of poverty, a 66.0 percent difference. The distribution was different for all people—12.3 percent were below 100 percent of poverty and 16.8 percent were below 125 percent of poverty, a 36.6 percent difference.

"The Census Bureau measure 'no longer provides an accurate picture of the differences in the extent of economic poverty among population groups or geographic areas.'"

Census Bureau Methods of Measuring Poverty Are Unreliable

John Cassidy

In the following viewpoint, business journalist John Cassidy argues that the Census Bureau's absolute definition of poverty— counting people as poor if their income falls below a calculated subsistence dollar level—is inaccurate and invalid. Cassidy contends that the bureau's poverty figures could be too low or too high: too low because the poverty thresholds underestimate the actual costs of housing and child care, too high because they count people whose income is only temporarily low, such as during a brief period of unemployment. He suggests that "relative deprivation" is a better measure: What matters is "how poor families make out compared with everybody else, not their abso-

John Cassidy, "Relatively Deprived," *New Yorker*, April 3, 2006, pp. 42–47. Copyright © 2006. All rights reserved. Reproduced by permission.

lute living standards." John Cassidy is a staff writer for the New Yorker *magazine and the author of* Dot.con: The Greatest Story Ever Sold.

As you read, consider the following questions:

1. How did Mollie Orshansky devise the formula by which the Census Bureau calculates the U.S. poverty rate today, according to Cassidy?
2. How does Cassidy answer the charge that a family can still qualify as poor if its members own stereos, dishwashers, color TVs, and Nintendo game systems?
3. What does the author suggest would be a simple method of calculating relative-poverty thresholds instead of the current absolute-poverty thresholds?

In the summer of 1963, Mollie Orshansky, a thirty-eight-year-old statistician at the Social Security Administration, in Washington, D.C., published an article in the *Social Security Bulletin* entitled "Children of the Poor." "The wonders of science and technology applied to a generous endowment of natural resources have wrought a way of life our grandfathers never knew," she wrote. "Creature comforts once the hallmark of luxury have descended to the realm of the commonplace, and the marvels of modern industry find their way into the home of the American worker as well as that of his boss. Yet there is an underlying disquietude reflected in our current social literature, an uncomfortable realization that an expanding economy has not brought gains to all in equal measure. It is reflected in the preoccupation with counting the poor—do they number 30 million, 40 million, or 50 million?"

Orshansky's timing was propitious. In December of 1962, President John F. Kennedy had asked Walter Heller, the chairman of the Council of Economic Advisers, to gather statistics on poverty. In early 1963, Heller gave the President a copy of a review by Dwight Macdonald, in *The New Yorker*, of Michael

Harrington's "The Other America: Poverty in the United States," in which Harrington claimed that as many as fifty million Americans were living in penury.

The federal government had never attempted to count the poor, and Orshansky's paper proposed an ingenious and straightforward way of doing so. . . .

Minimum Income Needed to Survive

In 1958, Orshansky joined the research department of the Social Security Administration, and decided to try to estimate the incidence of child poverty. "Poor people are everywhere; yet they are invisible," she told a reporter for the Dallas *Morning News* in 1999. "I wanted them to be seen clearly by those who make decisions about their lives." Building on pioneering research on diet and poverty conducted in York at the turn of the twentieth century by Seebohm Rowntree, a British social reformer, Orshanky used her food plans to calculate a subsistence budget for families of various sizes. For a mother and father with two children, she estimated the expense of a "low cost" plan at $3.60 a day, and of an even more frugal "economy plan" at $2.80 a day. Rather than trying to calculate the price of other items in the family budget, such as rent, heat, and clothing, Orshansky relied on a survey by the Agriculture Department, which showed that the typical American family spent about a third of its income on food. Thus, to determine the minimum income a family needed in order to survive, she simply multiplied the annual cost of the food plans by three. Families on the low-cost plan needed to earn at least $3,955 a year; families on the economy plan needed to earn $3,165.

Orshansky compared these figures with the Census Bureau's records on pre-tax family incomes and concluded that twenty-six per cent of families with children earned less than the upper poverty threshold and eighteen per cent earned less than the lower poverty threshold. In total, she estimated that between fifteen million and twenty-two million children were living in poverty, a disproportionate number of them in single-parent households and minority neighborhoods. "It would be one thing if poverty hit at random, and no one group were singled out," she wrote. "It is another thing to realize that some seem destined to poverty almost from birth—by their color or by the economic status or occupation of their parents."

Heller and his colleagues on the Council of Economic Advisers cited Orshansky's paper in an "Economic Report to the President" that appeared in January, 1964, shortly after Kennedy's successor, Lyndon B. Johnson, declared a "war on poverty" in his State of the Union address. In August of that year, Congress created the Office of Equal Opportunity, which used Orshansky's method to determine eligibility for new anti-poverty programs, such as Head Start. Other federal agencies followed suit, and in 1969 the White House adopted a slightly modified version of Orshansky's lower threshold—the one based on the economy food plan—as the official poverty line.

Shortcomings of Orshansky's Formula

In the nineteen-sixties, many economists believed that economic growth and government intervention would eliminate poverty. Between 1964 and 1973, as Johnson's Great Society programs went into effect, the poverty rate fell from nineteen per cent of the population to 11.1 per cent. But, while the nation's inflation-adjusted gross domestic product has virtually tripled since 1973, the poverty rate has hardly budged. In 2004, the most recent year for which figures are available, it stood at 12.7 per cent, a slight increase over the previous year, and in some regions the figure is much higher. The horror of Hurricane Katrina was not just the physical destruction it wrought but the economic hardship it exposed. In New Orleans, the poverty rate in 2004 was twenty-three per cent, a fact that George W. Bush noted in his address from New

Orleans' French Quarter on September 15th, when he said, "We have a duty to confront this poverty with bold action." . . . According to the Census Bureau, many cities are even poorer than New Orleans. In Detroit in 2004, the poverty rate was 33.6 per cent; in Miami, it was 28.3 per cent; and in Philadelphia it was 24.9 per cent. (In New York, it was 20.3 per cent.)

The persistence of endemic poverty raises questions about how poverty is measured. In the past ten years or so, significant changes have been made in the way that inflation, gross domestic product, and other economic statistics are derived, but the poverty rate is still calculated using the technique that Orshansky invented. (Every twelve months, the Census Bureau raises the income cutoffs slightly to take inflation into account.)

This approach has some obvious shortcomings. To begin with, the poverty thresholds are based on pre-tax income, which means that they don't take into account tax payments and income from anti-poverty programs, such as food stamps, housing subsidies, the Earned Income Tax Credit, and Medicaid, which cost taxpayers hundreds of billions of dollars a year. In addition, families' financial burdens have changed considerably since Orshansky conducted her research. In the late fifties, most mothers didn't have jobs outside the home, and they cooked their families' meals. Now that most mothers work full time and pay people to help them take care of their kids, child care and commuting consume more of a typical family budget.

Another problem is that the poverty thresholds are set at the same level all across the country. [In 2005], the pre-tax-income cutoff for a couple with two children was $19,806. This might be enough to support a family of four in rural Arkansas or Tennessee, but not in San Francisco, Boston, or New York, where the real-estate boom has created a shortage of affordable housing. According to Jared Bernstein and Lawrence Mishel, economists at the liberal Economic Policy Institute, in

Washington, D.C., the average rent in working-class neighborhoods of Boston is about a thousand dollars a month, which for a family of four with a poverty-level income leaves just six hundred and fifty dollars a month for food, clothing, heat, and everything else. Bernstein and Mishel argue that in some cities the poverty thresholds should be twice their current level.

Understating the Extent of Poverty

Such considerations suggest that the official measures understate the extent of poverty, but the opposite argument can also be made. The poverty figures fail to distinguish between temporary spells of hardship, like those caused by a job loss or a divorce, and long-term deprivation. Surveys show that as many as forty per cent of people who qualify as poor in any given year no longer do so the following year. Middle-class families that suffer a temporary loss of income can spend their savings, or take out a loan, to maintain their living standard, and they don't belong in the same category as the chronically impoverished. One way to remedy this problem is to consider how much households spend, rather than how much they earn. If in the course of a year a household spends less than some designated amount, it is classified as poor. Daniel T. Slesnick, an economist at the University of Texas, has tested this approach using figures that he obtained from the Department of Labor's Consumer Expenditure Survey, which tracks the buying habits of thousands of American families. Slesnick calculated that the "consumption poverty rate" for 1995—that is, the percentage of families whose spending was less than the poverty-income threshold—was 9.5 per cent, which is 4.3 per cent less than the official poverty rate. Subsequent studies have confirmed Slesnick's findings.

In 1995, a panel of experts assembled by the National Academy of Science concluded that the Census Bureau measure "no longer provides an accurate picture of the differences in the extent of economic poverty among population groups or geographic areas of the country, nor an accurate picture of trends over time." The panel recommended that the poverty line be revised to reflect taxes, benefits, child care, medical costs, and regional differences in prices. Statisticians at the Census Bureau have experimented with measures that incorporate some of these variables, but none of the changes have been officially adopted.

The obstacles are mainly political. "Poverty rates calculated using the experimental measures are all slightly higher than the official measure," Kathleen Short, John Iceland, and Joseph Dalaker, statisticians at the Census Bureau, reported in a 2002 paper reviewing the academy's recommendations. In addition to increasing the number of people officially classified as impoverished, revising the Census Bureau measure in the ways that the poverty experts suggested would mean that more elderly people and working families would be counted as poor.

Conservatives would prefer a measure that reduces the number of poor people. "The poverty rate misleads the public and our representatives, and it thereby degrades the quality of our social policies," Nicholas Eberstadt, of the American Enterprise Institute, wrote in a 2002 article. "It should be discarded for the broken tool that it is" In February [2006], the conservatives appeared to make some headway when the Census Bureau released a report on some new ways of measuring poverty that could cut the official rate by up to a third.

Deprivation Is Relative

Rather than trying to come up with a subsistence-based poverty measure about which everybody can agree, we should accept that there is no definitive way to decide who is impoverished and who isn't. Every three years, researchers from the federal government conduct surveys about the number of appliances in the homes of American families. In 2001, ninety-one per cent of poor families owned color televisions; seventy-four per cent owned microwave ovens; fifty-five per cent owned VCRs; and forty-seven per cent owned dishwashers. Are these families poverty-stricken?

Not according to W. Michael Cox, an economist at the Federal Reserve Bank of Dallas, and Richard Alm, a reporter at the Dallas *Morning News*. In their book "Myths of Rich and Poor: Why We're Better Off Than We Think" (1999), Cox and Alm argued that the poverty statistics overlook the extent to which falling prices have enabled poor families to buy consumer goods that a generation ago were considered luxury items. "By the standards of 1971, many of today's poor families might be considered members of the middle class," they wrote.

Consider a hypothetical single mother with two teenage sons living in New Orleans' Ninth Ward, a neighborhood with poor schools, high rates of crime and unemployment, and few opportunities for social advancement. The mother works four days a week in a local supermarket, where she makes eight dollars an hour. Her sons do odd jobs, earning a few hundred dollars a month, which they have used to buy stereo equipment, a DVD player, and a Nintendo. The family lives in public housing, and it qualifies for food stamps and Medicaid. Under the Earned Income Tax Credit program, the mother would receive roughly four thousand dollars from the federal government each year. Compared with the destitute in Africa and Asia, this family is unimaginably rich. Compared with a poor American family of thirty years ago, it may be slightly better off. Compared with a typical two-income family in the suburbs, it is poor. . . .

Disadvantages of Relative Deprivation

Although many poor families own appliances once associated with rich households, such as color televisions and dishwashers, they live in a society in which many families also possess DVD players, cell phones, desktop computers, broadband In-

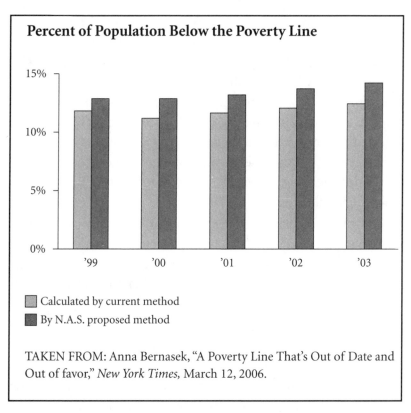

Percent of Population Below the Poverty Line

Calculated by current method

By N.A.S. proposed method

TAKEN FROM: Anna Bernasek, "A Poverty Line That's Out of Date and Out of favor," *New York Times*, March 12, 2006.

ternet connections, powerful game consoles, S.U.V.s, health-club memberships, and vacation homes. Without access to these goods, children from poor families may lack skills—such as how to surf the Web for help-wanted ads—that could enhance their prospects in the job market. In other words, relative deprivation may limit a person's capacity for social achievement. As [noted economist Amartya] Sen put it, "Being relatively poor in a rich country can be a great capability handicap, even when one's absolute income is high in terms of world standards." Research by Tom Hertz, an economist at American University, shows that a child whose parents are in the bottom fifth of the income distribution has only a six-percent chance of attaining an average yearly income in the top fifth. Most people who start out relatively poor stay relatively poor.

Since relative deprivation confers many of the disadvantages of absolute deprivation, it should be reflected in the poverty statistics. A simple way to do this would be to classify a household as impoverished if its pre-tax income was, say, less than half the median income—the income of the household at the center of the income-distribution curve. In 2004, the median pre-tax household income was $44,684; a poverty line based on relative deprivation would have been $22,342. (As under the current system, adjustments could be made for different family sizes.)

Adopting a relative-poverty threshold would put to rest the debate over how to define a subsistence threshold. As long as the new measure captured those at the bottom of the social hierarchy, it wouldn't matter much whether the income cutoff was set at forty per cent or fifty per cent of median income. If poverty is a relative phenomenon, what needs monitoring is how poor families make out compared with everybody else, not their absolute living standards.

Academics have proposed a relative-poverty line before; notably, the British sociologist Peter Townsend, in 1962, and the American economist Victor Fuchs, who is now an emeritus professor at Stanford, in 1965. Nobody has taken the idea very seriously. "I still think that it is the right way to think about poverty, especially from a policy point of view," Fuchs told me. Unfortunately, few politicians and poverty experts agree. Liberals fear that shifting the focus of policy away from hunger and physical need would make it even harder to win support for government anti-poverty programs; conservatives fear that adopting a relative-poverty rate would be tantamount to launching another costly war on poverty that the government couldn't hope to win.

A Relative-Poverty Line

Neither of these fears is justified. Many Americans are skeptical about government anti-poverty programs, because they believe that the impoverished bear some responsibility for their plight by dropping out of high school, taking drugs, or committing crimes. Raising public awareness about relative deprivation could help to change attitudes toward the poor, by showing how those at the bottom of the social hierarchy continue to face obstacles even as they, along with the rest of the society, become more prosperous. The *Times* recently reported that more than half of black men in inner cities fail to finish high school, and that, nationwide, almost three-quarters of black male high-school dropouts in their twenties are unemployed. "It doesn't do a poor person any good to say 'You are better off than you would have been thirty years ago,'" Fuchs said. "The pathologies we associate with poverty—crime, drug use, family disintegration—we haven't eliminated them at all."

The conservative case against a relative-poverty line asserts that since some people will always earn less than others the relative-poverty rate will never go down. Fortunately, this isn't necessarily true. If incomes were distributed more equally, fewer families would earn less than half the median income. Therefore, the way to reduce relative poverty is to reduce income inequality—perhaps by increasing the minimum wage and raising taxes on the rich. Between 1979 and 2000, the inflation-adjusted earnings of the poorest fifth of Americans increased just nine per cent; the earnings of the middle fifth rose fifteen per cent; and the earnings of the top fifth climbed sixty-eight per cent.

In the Ninth Ward and in neighborhoods like it, the gap between aspiration and reality has never been greater. As Americans were shocked to learn, many residents lacked the means to pay for transportation out of the city during Hurricane Katrina. But the poor of New Orleans were also relatively deprived, as became clear when they were transported to Houston and other cities and, in some cases, ended up staying with affluent white families. (Not surprisingly, conflict ensued. In Houston's public high schools, Katrina evacuees have been involved in brawls.) The entire episode demonstrated that those at the bottom of the social pecking order are not only economically detached from other Americans; they are also socially and geographically isolated.

Introducing a relative-poverty line would help shift attention to this larger problem of social exclusion. Although few attempts have been made to address the issue, the results have been promising. A recent long-term study of Head Start, which began in 1964, as one of the original "war on poverty" initiatives, found that poor children who participated in the program were more likely to finish high school and less likely to be arrested for committing crimes than those who did not. And in another initiative, undertaken between 1976 and 1998, the city of Chicago relocated thousands of impoverished African-Americans from inner-city projects to subsidized housing in middle-class, predominantly white suburbs; researchers found that the adults who participated were more likely to be employed, and their children were more likely to graduate from high school, than their inner-city counterparts. (A more recent experiment, in which the federal government gave vouchers to poor residents in a number of cities, enabling them to move to wealthier neighborhoods, has failed to produce similar gains. Many of the participants chose to live near one another, which researchers think may account for the disappointing results.)

Mollie Orshansky, who is now ninety-one and living on Manhattan's East Side, never warmed to the idea of a relative-poverty line—she was too concerned about people actually starving—but she wasn't wedded to her method, either. "If someone has a better approach, fine," she said in 1999. "I was working with what I had and with what I knew."

"Most of America's 'poor' live in material conditions that would be judged as comfortable or well-off just a few generations ago."

Most "Poor" Americans Enjoy a Comfortable Standard of Living

Robert Rector

Robert Rector is senior research fellow in domestic policy studies at the Heritage Foundation, a conservative think tank in Washington, D.C. In the following viewpoint, Rector disputes the popular perception that being poor in America means destitution. On the contrary, he argues, the average poor American has adequate food and nutrition, enjoys a wide range of material amenities, owns at least one car, and has more living space than the average citizen of major European cities. Rector concludes that the typical face of poverty is far from the dire images presented by the press and liberal politicians.

As you read, consider the following questions:

1. What percentage of poor households actually own their own homes, according to Rector?

Robert Rector, "How Poor Are America's Poor? Examining the 'Plague' of Poverty in America," *Heritage Foundation Backgrounder*, August 27, 2007. Copyright © 2007 The Heritage Foundation. Reproduced by permission.

2. What are the two main reasons children are poor in America, according to the author?

3. What does Rector cite as the primary nutrition-related health problem among the poor?

Poverty is an important and emotional issue. [In 2006] the Census Bureau released its annual report on poverty in the United States declaring that there were 37 million poor persons living in this country in 2005, roughly the same number as in the preceding years. According to the Census report, 12.6 percent of Americans were poor in 2005; this number has varied from 11.3 percent to 15.1 percent of the population over the past 20 years.

To understand poverty in America, it is important to look behind these numbers—to look at the actual living conditions of the individuals the government deems to be poor. For most Americans, the word "poverty" suggests destitution: an inability to provide a family with nutritious food, clothing, and reasonable shelter. But only a small number of the 37 million persons classified as "poor" by the Census Bureau fit that description. While real material hardship certainly does occur, it is limited in scope and severity. Most of America's "poor" live in material conditions that would be judged as comfortable or well-off just a few generations ago. Today, the expenditures per person of the lowest-income one-fifth (or quintile) of households equal those of the median American household in the early 1970s, after adjusting for inflation.

The Poor Are Far from Deprived

The following are facts about persons defined as "poor" by the Census Bureau, taken from various government reports:

- Forty-three percent of all poor households actually own their own homes. The average home owned by persons classified as poor by the Census Bureau is a three-bedroom house with one-and-a-half baths, a garage, and a porch or patio.

- Eighty percent of poor households have air conditioning. By contrast, in 1970, only 36 percent of the entire U.S. population enjoyed air conditioning.

- Only 6 percent of poor households are overcrowded. More than two-thirds have more than two rooms per person.

- The average poor American has more living space than the average individual living in Paris, London, Vienna, Athens, and other cities throughout Europe. (These comparisons are to the *average* citizens in foreign countries, not to those classified as poor.)

- Nearly three-quarters of poor households own a car; 31 percent own two or more cars.

- Ninety-seven percent of poor households have a color television; over half own two or more color televisions.

- Seventy-eight percent have a VCR or DVD player; 62 percent have cable or satellite TV reception.

- Eighty-nine percent own microwave ovens, more than half have a stereo, and more than a third have an automatic dishwasher.

As a group, America's poor are far from being chronically undernourished. The average consumption of protein, vitamins, and minerals is virtually the same for poor and middle-class children and, in most cases, is well above recommended norms. Poor children actually consume more meat than do higher-income children and have average protein intakes 100 percent above recommended levels. Most poor children today are, in fact, supernourished and grow up to be, on average, one inch taller and 10 pounds heavier than the GIs who stormed the beaches of Normandy in World War II.

While the poor are generally well nourished, some poor families do experience temporary food shortages. But even this condition is relatively rare; 89 percent of the poor report their families have "enough" food to eat, while only 2 percent say they "often" do not have enough to eat.

Overall, the typical American defined as poor by the government has a car, air conditioning, a refrigerator, a stove, a clothes washer and dryer, and a microwave. He has two color televisions, cable or satellite TV reception, a VCR or DVD player, and a stereo. He is able to obtain medical care. His home is in good repair and is not overcrowded. By his own report, his family is not hungry and he had sufficient funds in the past year to meet his family's essential needs. While this individual's life is not opulent, it is equally far from the popular images of dire poverty conveyed by the press, liberal activists, and politicians.

Hardships at the Lower Extreme

Of course, the living conditions of the average poor American should not be taken as representing all the poor. There is actually a wide range in living conditions among the poor. For example, a third of poor households have both cellular and landline telephones. A third also have telephone answering machines. At the other extreme, however, approximately one-tenth have no phone at all. Similarly, while the majority of poor households do not experience significant material problems, roughly 30 percent do experience at least one problem such as overcrowding, temporary hunger, or difficulty getting medical care.

The remaining poverty in the U.S. can be reduced further, particularly poverty among children. There are two main reasons that American children are poor: Their parents don't work much, and fathers are absent from the home.

In good economic times or bad, the typical poor family with children is supported by only 800 hours of work during a year: That amounts to 16 hours of work per week. If work in each family were raised to 2,000 hours per year—the equivalent of one adult working 40 hours per week through-out the year—nearly 75 percent of poor children would be lifted out of official poverty.

Father absence is another major cause of child poverty. Nearly two-thirds of poor children reside in single-parent homes; each year, an additional 1.5 million children are born out of wedlock. If poor mothers married the ·fathers of their children, almost three-quarters would immediately be lifted out of poverty. . . .

Property Ownership and Amenities

Some 43 percent of poor households own their own home. The typical home owned by the poor is a three-bedroom house with one-and-a-half baths. It has a garage or carport and a porch or patio and is located on a half-acre lot. The house was constructed in 1969 and is in good repair. The median value of homes owned by poor households was $95,276 in 2005 or 70 percent of the median value of all homes owned in the United States.

Some 73 percent of poor households own a car or truck; nearly a third own two or more cars or trucks. Eighty percent have air conditioning; by contrast, in 1970, only 36 percent of the general U.S. population had air conditioning. Nearly nine in ten poor households own microwaves; more than a third have automatic dishwashers.

Poor households are well equipped with modern enter-tainment technology. It should come as no surprise that nearly all (97 percent) poor households have color TVs, but more than half actually own two or more color televisions. One-quarter own large-screen televisions, 78 percent have a VCR or DVD player, and almost two-thirds have cable or satellite TV reception. Some 58 percent own a stereo.

More than a third of poor households have telephone an-swering machines. Roughly a third have both cell phones and conventional landline telephones. More than a third have personal computers. While these numbers do not suggest lives of luxury, they are notably different from conventional images of poverty. . . .

Poverty and Malnutrition

Malnutrition (also called undernutrition) is a condition of reduced health due to a chronic shortage of calories and nutriments. There is little or no evidence of poverty-induced malnutrition in the United States. It is often believed that a lack of financial resources forces poor people to eat low-quality diets that are deficient in nutriments and high in fat. However, survey data show that nutriment density (amount of vitamins, minerals, and protein per kilocalorie of food) does not vary by income class. Nor do the poor consume higher-fat diets than do the middle class; the percentage of persons with high fat intake (as a share of total calories) is virtually the same for low-income and upper-middle-income persons. Overconsumption of calories in general, however, is a major problem among the poor, as it is within the general U.S. population. . . .

The principal nutrition-related health problem among the poor, as with the general U.S. population, stems from the *over*consumption, not under-consumption, of food. While overweight and obesity are prevalent problems throughout the U.S. population, they are found most frequently among poor adults. Poor adult men are slightly less likely than non-poor men to be overweight (30.4 percent compared to 31.9 percent); but . . . poor adult women are significantly more likely to be overweight than are non-poor women (47.3 percent compared to 32 percent). . . .

Government data show that most poor households do not suffer even from temporary food shortages. Overall, . . . 98 percent of U.S. households report that they always had "enough food to eat" during the past four months, although not always the kinds of food they would have preferred. Some

U.S. Poverty Statistics Are Inflated

Except for people who can't work or won't work, there is very little real poverty in the United States today, except among people who come from poverty-stricken countries and bring their poverty with them. . . .

The Left has striven mightily to make working no longer necessary for having a claim to a share of what others have produced—whether a share of "the nation's" wealth or "the world's" wealth.

They have also striven mightily to inflate the number of people who look poor by counting young people with entry-level jobs, who are passing through lower income brackets at the beginning of their careers, among "the poor," even though most of these young people have incomes above the national average when they are older.

Thomas Sowell, National Review Online,
December 28, 2006.

1.8 percent of all households report they "sometimes" did not have enough food to eat during the previous four months, while 0.4 percent say they "often" did not have enough food.

Among the poor, the figures are only slightly lower: 92.5 percent of poor households assert that they always had "enough food to eat" during the previous four months, although 26 percent of these did not always have the foods they would have preferred. Some 6 percent of poor households state that they "sometimes" did not have enough food and 1.5 percent say they "often" did not have enough food. The bottom line: Although a small portion of poor households report temporary food shortages, the overwhelming majority of poor households report that they consistently have enough food to eat. . . .

Living Conditions and Hardships

Overall, the living standards of most poor Americans are far higher than is generally appreciated. The overwhelming majority of poor families are well housed, have adequate food, and enjoy a wide range of modern amenities, including air conditioning and cable television. Some 70 percent of poor households report that during the course of the past year they were able to meet "all essential expenses," including mortgage, rent, utility bills, and important medical care. . . .

However, two caveats should be applied to this generally optimistic picture. First, many poor families have difficulty paying their regular bills and must scramble to make ends meet. For example, more than a third of poor families are late in paying the rent or utility bills at some point during the year.

Second, the living conditions of the average poor household should not be taken to represent all poor households. There is a wide range of living conditions among the poor: a third of poor households have both cell phones and landline phones; a third also have telephone answering machines. But, at the other extreme, a tenth of the poor have no telephone at all. Similarly, most of America's poor live in accommodations with two or more rooms per person, but around 7 percent of the poor are crowded, with less than one room per person. . . .

Overall, Hardship Is Not Widespread

Altogether, around 62 percent of poor households experienced no . . . financial or physical hardships. These families were able to pay all their bills on time. They were able to obtain medical care if needed, had enough food, were not crowded, and had few upkeep problems in the home. Another 17 percent of poor households experienced one financial or material problem during the year. Around 21 percent of poor households had two or more financial or material problems.

The most common problem facing poor households was late payment of rent or utilities. While having difficulty paying monthly bills is stressful, in most cases late payment did not result in material hardship or deprivation. Relatively few of those who were late in payments subsequently had their utilities cut off or were evicted. If late payment problems are excluded from the count, we find that 71 percent of poor households had no ... remaining problems. Some 18 percent had one problem, and 11 percent had two or more problems.

While it is appropriate to be concerned about the difficulties faced by some poor families, it is important to keep these problems in perspective. Many poor families have intermittent difficulty paying rent or utility bills but remain very well housed by historic or international standards. Even poor families, who are overcrowded by U.S. standards or face temporary food shortages, are still likely to have living conditions that are far above the world average.

"A quarter of the workforce . . . earn less
than . . . $18,800 a year—the income
that marks the federal poverty line for
a family of four."

The Working Poor Are Not Getting By in America

Michelle Conlin and Aaron Bernstein

*In the following viewpoint, Michelle Conlin and Aaron Bernstein
examine the plight of more than 28 million Americans who constitute the working poor—employed but typically for low hourly
wages without health care, pensions, paid sick days, or other
benefits. Climbing up the economic ladder, even in a robust
economy, is increasingly difficult, the authors argue, against the
downward pressures of globalization and corporate cost-cutting
and the decline of labor unions. In this atmosphere of maximum
job insecurity, they maintain, "one missed bus, one stalled engine, one sick kid means the difference" between subsistence and
poverty. Michelle Conlin is a senior writer and editor of the
Working Life Department at* Business Week *magazine in New
York City. Aaron Bernstein is a senior writer on workplace and
social issues in* Business Week's *Washington, DC, bureau.*

As you read, consider the following questions:

1. According to Conlin and Bernstein, what percentage of families below the federal poverty line have one or more workers?

2. Why will fast growth of several occupations in which the working poor are concentrated be unlikely to improve their prospects, according to the authors?

3. In what way are people who push themselves to earn more than a poverty-level wage even worse off, in the authors' view?

Katrina Gill, a 36-year-old certified nursing aide, worked in one of the premiere long-term care facilities near Portland, Ore. From 10:30 p.m. to 7 a.m., she was on duty alone, performing three rounds on the dementia ward, where she took care of up to 28 patients a night for $9.32 an hour. She monitored vitals, turned for bedsores, and changed adult diapers. There were the constant vigils over patients like the one who would sneak into other rooms, mistaking female patients for his deceased wife. Worse was the resident she called "the hitter" who once lunged at her, ripping a muscle in her back and laying her flat for four days.

[In April 2004] Gill quit and took another job for 68 cents an hour more, bringing her salary to $14,400 a year. But like so many health-care workers, she has no health-care benefits from her job. So she and her garage mechanic husband pay $640 monthly for a policy and have racked up $160,000 in medical debts from their youngest son Brandyn's cancer care.

In New York City, Joseph Schiraldi, 41, guards one of the biggest terrorist targets in the world: the Empire State Building. For eight hours a day, he X-rays packages, checks visitors' IDs, and patrols the concourse. But on $7.50 an hour in the priciest city in the U.S., he's a security officer without security—no pension, no health care, and no paid sick days, typical for a nonunion guard.

Bellingham (Wash.) day-care teacher Mandy Smith can't afford child care for her 6-year-old son, Jordan, on her take-home pay of $60 a day. Neither can commercial cleaner Theresa Fabre on her $8.50 an hour job. So her son, Christian, 9, waits for her after school in a crumbling upper Manhattan library where the kids line up five-deep to use one of two computers. The librarian doubles as a de facto babysitter for 40 or so other kids of the working poor. . . .

The loss of lucrative white-collar work offshore has dominated news headlines, provoking economic anxiety among middle-class families who fear they may be next. But there's an equally troubling yet more often overlooked problem among the nation's working poor—for whom the raises come in dimes, the sick days go unpaid, and the benefits are out of reach.

Today more than 28 million people, about a quarter of the workforce between the ages of 18 and 64, earn less than $9.04 an hour, which translates into a full-time salary of $18,800 a year—the income that marks the federal poverty line for a family of four. Any definition of the working poor, of course, involves some blurry lines. Some, like Gill, who make just above the $9.04 wage, often bounce around the threshold with their chaotic hours, slippery job security, and tumultuous lives.

There's also the fact that about one-third work only part-time, and more than a third are 18- to 25-year-olds, who may still live at home but may eventually work their way up the ladder. Some perhaps moonlight with a second job. And others may have spouses whose incomes lift their families up. But most poor workers tend to marry people with similar backgrounds, leaving both to juggle jobs as janitors, health aides, and retail workers that don't raise them into the middle class.

Overall, 63% of U.S. families below the federal poverty line have one or more workers, according to the Census Bureau. They're not just minorities, either; nearly 60% are white.

About a fifth of the working poor are foreign-born, mostly from Mexico. And the majority possess high school diplomas and even some college—which 30 years ago would virtually have assured them a shot at the middle class.

Toil and Trouble

Now, though, most labor in a netherworld of maximum insecurity, where one missed bus, one stalled engine, one sick kid means the difference between keeping a job and getting fired, between subsistence and setting off the financial tremors of turned-off telephones and $1,000 emergency-room bills that can bury them in a mountain of subprime debt.

At any moment, a boss pressured to pump profits can slash hours, shortchanging a family's grocery budget—or conversely, force employees to work off the clock, wreaking havoc on child-care plans. Often, as they get close to putting in enough time to qualify for benefits, many see their schedules cut back. The time it takes to don uniforms, go to the bathroom, or take breaks routinely goes unpaid. Complain, and there is always someone younger, cheaper, and newer to the U.S. willing to do the work for less. Pittsburgh native Edward Plesniak, 36, lost his $10.68-an-hour union job as a janitor when the contractor fired all the union workers to make way for cheaper, nonunion labor. So far, Plesniak has been able to dredge up work only as a part-time floor waxer. The pay: $6.00 an hour, with no benefits. "I feel like I'm in a nightmare," says the married father of three. "And I can't wake up."

What's happening in the world's richest, most powerful country when so many families seem to be struggling? And what can be done? There's no question that robust growth is a potent remedy: Recall that the full-employment economy of the late 1990s reduced the ranks of the working poor. Five years of a 4% jobless rate bid up wages across the board. That brought a healthy cumulative 14% pay hike, after inflation, to those in the bottom fifth between 1995 and 2003, when they averaged $8.46 an hour, according to an analysis of Census data by the Economic Policy Institute (EPI), a liberal Washington research group. The share of the workforce earning subpoverty pay actually shrank eight percentage points, to 24% [in 2003], or 5 million fewer than in 1995.

That's real progress, certainly. But it still leaves many workers earning less than what it takes to lift a family above the poverty line. In other words, the boom didn't last long enough to bring more people into better circumstances. Now, in the current recovery, there has been brisk growth again, as well as high productivity and job creation. But so far, wages at the low end haven't budged much. Many of today's economic gains are flowing to profits and efficiency improvements, and the job market isn't tight enough yet to lift pay for average workers, much less for those on the bottom. . . .

Perplexing, too, are signs that many jobs the working poor hold won't, over time, lead them out of their straits. Five of the 10 fastest-growing occupations over the next decade will be of the menial, dead-end variety, including retail clerks, janitors, and cashiers, according to the Bureau of Labor Statistics. What's more, while full employment in the 1990s may have brought higher pay for people like health aides and maids, the ladder up into the middle class has gotten longer, and they are more likely than in other periods to remain a health aide or a maid.

A 2003 study of 1990s mobility by two economists at the Federal Reserve Bank of Boston found that the chances that poor Americans would stay stuck in their strata had increased vs. the 1970s. Given the economy's strong showing in the '90s, that's a concern. "If current trends persist, a greater and greater share of wealth will keep going into the hands of the few, which will destroy initiative," worries James D. Sinegal, CEO of Costco Wholesale Corp., which offers above-average pay and benefits in the retail sector. "We'll no longer have a motivated working class."

So although a fast-growing economy and full employment are necessary for powering wages at the bottom, they may not be enough in today's economy. To survive in waves of increasing global competition, U.S. companies have relentlessly cut costs and sought maximum productivity. That has put steady downward pressure particularly on the lowest rungs of the labor force, while rewarding the growing ranks of educated knowledge workers. In this increasingly bifurcated job market, workers who lack skills and training have seen their bargaining power crumble relative to those higher up the scale.

For one thing, globalization has thrown the least-skilled into head-on competition with people willing to work for pennies on the dollar. And a torrent of immigration, mainly poor rural Mexicans, has further swelled the low-end labor pool. Together, these trends have shoved many hourly wage occupations into a worldwide, discount labor store stocked with cheap temps, hungry part-timers, and dollar-a-day labor in India, Mexico, and China, all willing to sell their services to the lowest bidder. Against such headwinds, full employment offers only partial protection.

What's more, other traditional buffers don't help low-end workers as much anymore. While labor unions were largely responsible for creating the broad middle class after World War II, bringing decent wages and benefits to even low-skilled employees such as hotel and garment workers, that's not the case today. Most U.S. employers fiercely resist unionization, which, along with other factors, has helped slash union membership to just 13% of the workforce, vs. a midcentury peak of more than 35%.

Gravitational Pressure

The federal minimum wage, too, long served as a bulwark against low pay by putting a floor under the bottom as the rest of the workforce gained ground. At $5.15 an hour, it re-

mains 30% less than it was in 1968, after inflation adjustments. [The minimum wage was raised to $5.85 per hour in
July 2007.]

Add to all this the fact that a college degree, the time-
tested passport to success, is today less available to those without family resources. The cost of college has exploded, leaving
fewer than 5% of students from bottom-earning families able
to get that all-important diploma. The result: The pattern of
low skills crosses the generations. Columbus Harris, 50, a
$6.75-an-hour driver for the elderly in Pine Bluff, Ark.,
couldn't help his kids with college. So his middle son Christopher joined the Army to get an education. "I worry about the
fact that a lot of the gains in educational attainment are concentrated among the youngsters from rich and upper-middle-
class families," says Gary Burtless, a senior fellow at the Brookings Institution.

There are no easy policy prescriptions for improving the
working poor's prospects. Measures with any real impact are
almost always costly and ignite political fights over priorities.
Lifting the minimum wage [to $6.65] an hour, for example,
would boost the incomes of more than 10 million workers. A
majority of the gains would flow to adult women over age 20,
mostly nonunionized workers in retail, according to an analysis by the EPI. To support the wage floor over the long term,
the minimum would need to be linked to some measure of
national living standards, such as inflation or average wages,
to keep many families from simply slipping back into working
poverty after a few years. Yet trying to hike the minimum
wage always sparks a monumental battle in Washington. That's
just [what happened], after Senator Edward M. Kennedy (D.-
Mass.) proposed to lift it to $7.00 an hour.

Writing some new rules for globalization would shore up
low-end workers, too. Some Democrats advocate linking trade
pacts to labor rights, by, for example, requiring countries that
want favored trade status to allow workers to form unions.

Hard Work Is No Longer the Ticket Out of Poverty

In America, to be poor is a stigma. In a country which celebrates individuality and the goal of giving everyone an equal opportunity to make it big, those in poverty are often blamed for their own situation. Experience on the ground does little to bear that out. When people are working two jobs at a time and still failing to earn enough to feed their families, it seems impossible to call them lazy or selfish. There seems to be a failure in the system, not the poor themselves.

It is an impression backed up by many of those mired in poverty in Oklahoma and Kentucky. Few asked for handouts. Many asked for decent wages. . . . But the economy does not seem to be allowing people to make a decent living. It condemns the poor to stay put, fighting against seemingly impossible odds or to pull up sticks and try somewhere else.

Paul Harris, Guardian Unlimited, *February 19, 2006.*

The idea isn't to eliminate low-wage competition—an impossibility, in any case—but simply to blunt its sharpest blows, particularly on less-skilled, predominantly male factory workers. Many economists calculate that globalization has been responsible for about one-fifth of the decline in blue-collar pay since 1973. But just think back to the fight over NAFTA [North American Free Trade Agreement] a decade ago to see how far such proposals might go in Congress.

Curbing the flood of unskilled immigrants, assuming it could even be done, also would ease some of the gravitational pressure on low-end pay. Slowing the pace of entry, or shifting the flow toward higher-skilled workers, would mitigate the stiff wage competition among everyone from janitors to sales clerks. Yet if anything, political momentum seems to be moving in the opposite direction, such as President Bush's proposals earlier this year to set up a temporary worker program.

A hike in unionization would also give the working poor some leverage over wages. The rule of thumb used to be that union workers earn about one-third more than nonunion ones. But the differential has ballooned with the collapse of pay scales at the bottom. Today, blue-collar workers in a union make 54% more than unorganized ones and are more than twice as likely to have health insurance and pensions, according to an EPI analysis. Because unions boost workers' bargaining power and help them win a greater share of productivity gains, any resurgence would give low-wage workers more clout to deal with the effects of factors such as globalization, immigration, and technology. Still, the U.S. isn't likely to alter the laws governing unionization any time soon. Employers have body-blocked such attempts since the late 1970s, arguing that profits and economic growth would suffer. Today, labor law reform still goes nowhere, snagged in the broader political deadlock that grips the U.S. . . .

Where Hope Lies

Still, historically, class-based appeals have had scant resonance in U.S. politics. In addition, there's little sustained outcry from the working poor themselves, who often are overwhelmed by their personal difficulties and politically disengaged. Only about 40% of them vote, vs. 74% of the investor class, according to the Russell Sage Foundation. "If you look at families in the bottom 20%, they are dropping out of the political system like flies," says foundation President Eric Wanner.

A few initiatives, though, have broad enough appeal to win support from both sides of the divide. Lawmakers from both political parties are struggling to devise ways to help the uninsured get health coverage. While they're split on this subject, too, nearly everyone agrees that something should be done. The Children's Health Insurance Program (CHIP), which covers poor kids, was established by Democrats and Republicans alike, though a lot of children remain uncovered. Any expansion, or a broader solution that involves expanding Medicaid, would help many working poor adults, among the most likely to need coverage. . . .

Still, even those who push above a poverty-level wage can fall into a trap. Between $7 to $10 an hour, they make just enough to start losing what little safely net there is, says Ron Haskins, a former Republican staffer who helped spearhead the 1996 welfare reform, now a senior fellow at the Brookings Institution. They often become ineligible for food stamps or child-care assistance, and the earned income tax credit starts phasing out for a single parent at $13,730. "For them, Horatio Alger [a literary character who worked his way up from poverty] does not apply," says Haskins.

Women, especially single ones, have the most difficulty. Often, their wages barely cover the cost of child care. Low-income women's pay is actually up since 1973, but they still average just $7.94 an hour, much less than their male counterparts. That's one reason the U.S. has the highest child-poverty rate in the industrialized world. "Our low-income mothers work twice as hard as those in any other industrial country—but their kids are the worst off," says Syracuse University public policy professor Timothy M. Smeeding.

The Wal-Mart Effect

Lately, there's a new name for the downward pressure on wages: the so-called Wal-Martization of the economy. Most recently, the dynamic played out starkly in the five-month Southern California supermarket strike that ended in February [2004]. The three chains involved, Safeway, Albertson's, and Kroger, said they had no choice but to cut pay and benefits drastically now that 40 Wal-Mart Stores supercenters would be opening up in the area. The reason: Wal-Mart pays its full-time hourly workers an average of $9.64, about a third less than the level of the union chains. It also shoulders much less of its workers' annual health insurance costs than rivals, leaving 53% of its 1.2 million employees uncovered by the company plan.

Now, after the strike, new hires will have lower wages and bear a much higher share of health costs than current union members, making health insurance too pricey for many of them, too. Eventually, many grocery jobs could wind up paying poverty-level wages, just like Wal-Mart's. "I used to load workers into my truck to take them down to United Way," says Jon Lehman, a former manager of a Louisville Wal-Mart who now works for the United Food & Commercial Workers Union. In his 17 years with Wal-Mart, he kept a Rolodex with numbers for homeless shelters, food banks, and soup kitchens. "They couldn't make it on their paychecks."

It's a prospect that deeply worries workers like Sherry Kovas. Over 26 years, she worked her way up to $17.90 an hour as a cashier at Ralph's Grocery Co. store in the posh California enclave of Indian Wells. To Kovas, the Medici-like lifestyles of her customers—the personal chefs, the necklaces that would pay her yearly salary—never seemed so much an emblem of inequality as a symbol of what was possible. Now, though, after the banks foreclosed on some strikers' homes and the repo men hauled away their cars, there's already talk of grocery store closings in the area because of the new Wal-Mart supercenter up the road. "They say Wal-Mart's going to kill us," says Kovas, who fears losing the three-bedroom modular home that she, her five-year-old son, husband, and mother-in-law share. "But I'm 44 years old. I'm too old to start over."

The U.S. has long tolerated wider disparities in income than other industrialized countries, mostly out of a belief that anyone with enough moxie and hustle could lift themselves up in America's vibrant economy. Sadly, it seems that path is becoming an ever steeper climb. Strong recovery and vigorous growth will again get wages growing. But as a new phase of prosperity begins, it may be time for some added advantages for those struggling in a brutal global economy. Otherwise, the outcome could be more polarization and inequality. The farther down that road the country goes, the harder it will be to change course.

| "The number of severely poor Americans grew by 26 percent from 2000 to 2005."

Record Numbers of Americans Are Abjectly Poor

Tony Pugh

Nearly 16 million Americans live in deep poverty, Tony Pugh claims in the following viewpoint, and the number of abjectly poor people—those whose annual income is less than half of the Census Bureau poverty line—is growing faster than any other segment of the poor population. According to Pugh, although the percentage of African Americans in deep poverty is more than three times higher than the percentage of non-Hispanic whites in deep poverty, most of the poorest of the poor are female and white, with children. The vast majority, he states, are not recipients of welfare benefits, either because they have exhausted their eligibility or because they fall between the cracks of federal assistance programs. Tony Pugh has reported on consumer economics for the McClatchy Newspapers' Washington Bureau since 1997.

As you read, consider the following questions:

1. As cited by Pugh, in which regions and cities is severe poverty worst?

2. According to VCU researcher Steven Woolf, quoted by the author, what is "the sinkhole effect"?

3. According to professor Mark Rank, as cited by Pugh, how many Americans will experience at least a year of severe poverty in their lifetime?

Washington – The percentage of poor Americans who are living in severe poverty has reached a 32-year high, millions of working Americans are falling closer to the poverty line and the gulf between the nation's "haves" and "have-nots" continues to widen.

A McClatchy Newspapers analysis of 2005 census figures, the latest available, found that nearly 16 million Americans are living in deep or severe poverty. A family of four with two children and an annual income of less than $9,903—half the federal poverty line—was considered severely poor in 2005. So were individuals who made less than $5,080 a year.

The McClatchy analysis found that the number of severely poor Americans grew by 26 percent from 2000 to 2005. That's 56 percent faster than the overall poverty population grew in the same period. McClatchy's review also found statistically significant increases in the percentage of the population in severe poverty in 65 of 215 large U.S. counties, and similar increases in 28 states. The review also suggested that the rise in severely poor residents isn't confined to large urban counties but extends to suburban and rural areas.

The plight of the severely poor is a distressing sidebar to an unusual economic expansion. Worker productivity has increased dramatically since the brief recession of 2001, but wages and job growth have lagged behind. At the same time, the share of national income going to corporate profits has dwarfed the amount going to wages and salaries. That helps explain why the median household income of working-age families, adjusted for inflation, has fallen for five straight years.

These and other factors have helped push 43 percent of the nation's 37 million poor people into deep poverty—the highest rate since at least 1975.

The share of poor Americans in deep poverty has climbed slowly but steadily over the last three decades. But since 2000, the number of severely poor has grown "more than any other segment of the population," according to a recent study in the *American Journal of Preventive Medicine.*

"That was the exact opposite of what we anticipated when we began," said Dr. Steven Woolf of Virginia Commonwealth University, who co-authored the study. "We're not seeing as much moderate poverty as a proportion of the population. What we're seeing is a dramatic growth of severe poverty."

The growth spurt, which leveled off in 2005, in part reflects how hard it is for low-skilled workers to earn their way out of poverty in an unstable job market that favors skilled and educated workers. It also suggests that social programs aren't as effective as they once were at catching those who fall into economic despair.

About one in three severely poor people are under age 17, and nearly two out of three are female. Female-headed families with children account for a large share of the severely poor.

According to census data, nearly two of three people in severe poverty are white (10.3 million) and 6.9 million are non-Hispanic whites. Severely poor blacks (4.3 million) are more than three times as likely as non-Hispanic whites to be in deep poverty, while extremely poor Hispanics of any race (3.7 million) are more than twice as likely.

Washington, D.C., the nation's capital, has a higher concentration of severely poor people—10.8 percent in 2005—than any of the 50 states, topping even hurricane-ravaged

Mississippi and Louisiana, with 9.3 percent and 8.3 percent, respectively. Nearly six of 10 poor District residents are in extreme poverty.

'I Don't Ask for Nothing'

A few miles from the Capitol Building, 60-year-old John Treece pondered his life in deep poverty as he left a local food pantry with two bags of free groceries.

Plagued by arthritis, back problems and myriad ailments from years of manual labor, Treece has been unable to work full time for 15 years. He's tried unsuccessfully to get benefits from the Social Security Administration, which he said disputes his injuries and work history.

In 2006, an extremely poor individual earned less than $5,244 a year, according to federal poverty guidelines. Treece said he earned about that much in 2006 doing odd jobs.

Wearing shoes with holes, a tattered plaid jacket and a battered baseball cap, Treece lives hand-to-mouth in a $450-a-month room in a nondescript boarding house in a high-crime neighborhood. Thanks to food stamps, the food pantry and help from relatives, Treece said he never goes hungry. But toothpaste, soap, toilet paper and other items that require cash are tougher to come by.

"Sometimes it makes you want to do the wrong thing, you know," Treece said, referring to crime. "But I ain't a kid no more. I can't do no time. At this point, I ain't got a lotta years left."

Treece remains positive and humble despite his circumstances.

"I don't ask for nothing," he said. "I just thank the Lord for this day and ask that tomorrow be just as blessed."

Like Treece, many who did physical labor during their peak earning years have watched their job prospects dim as their bodies gave out.

David Jones, the president of the Community Service Society of New York City, an advocacy group for the poor, testified before the House Ways and Means Committee [in January 2007] that he was shocked to discover how pervasive the problem was.

"You have this whole cohort of, particularly African-Americans of limited skills, men, who can't participate in the workforce because they don't have skills to do anything but heavy labor," he said.

'A Permanent Underclass'

Severe poverty is worst near the Mexican border and in some areas of the South, where 6.5 million severely poor residents are struggling to find work as manufacturing jobs in the textile, apparel and furniture-making industries disappear. The Midwestern Rust Belt and areas of the Northeast also have been hard hit as economic restructuring and foreign competition have forced numerous plant closings.

At the same time, low-skilled immigrants with impoverished family members are increasingly drawn to the South and Midwest to work in the meatpacking, food processing and agricultural industries.

These and other factors such as increased fluctuations in family incomes and illegal immigration have helped push 43 percent of the nation's 37 million poor people into deep poverty—the highest rate in at least 32 years.

"What appears to be taking place is that, over the long term, you have a significant permanent underclass that is not being impacted by anti-poverty policies," said Michael Tanner, the director of Health and Welfare Studies at the Cato Institute, a libertarian think tank.

Arloc Sherman, a senior researcher at the Center on Budget and Policy Priorities, a liberal think tank, disagreed. "It doesn't look like a growing permanent underclass," said Sherman, whose organization has chronicled the growth of deep poverty. "What you see in the data are more and more single moms with children who lose their jobs and who aren't being caught by a safety net anymore."

About 1.1 million such families account for roughly 2.1 million deeply poor children, Sherman said.

After fleeing an abusive marriage in 2002, 42-year-old Marjorie Sant moved with her three children from Arkansas to a seedy boarding house in Raleigh, N.C., where the four shared one bedroom. For most of 2005, they lived off food stamps and the $300 a month in Social Security Disability Income for her son with attention deficit hyperactivity disorder. Teachers offered clothes to Sant's children. Saturdays meant lunch at the Salvation Army.

"To depend on other people to feed and clothe your kids is horrible," Sant said. "I found myself in a hole and didn't know how to get out."

In the summer of 2005, social workers warned that she'd lose her children if her home situation didn't change. Sant then brought her two youngest children to a temporary housing program at the Raleigh Rescue Mission while her oldest son moved to California to live with an adult daughter from a previous marriage.

So for 10 months, Sant learned basic office skills. She now lives in a rented house, works two jobs and earns about $20,400 a year.

Sant is proud of where she is, but she knows that "if something went wrong, I could well be back to where I was."

'I'm Getting Nowhere Fast'

As more poor Americans sink into severe poverty, more individuals and families living within $8,000 above or below the poverty line also have seen their incomes decline. Steven Woolf of Virginia Commonwealth University attributes this to what he calls a "sinkhole effect" on income.

Living on $5,250 a Year

The $5,250 for an abjectly poor individual means a bare bones budget of $437/month. Of that total, no more than $50 is available per week for food, or $7.14 day—about two big Macs and a drink, or 1200–1600 calories a day and 120 grams of fat. The residual income supports a housing expenditure in the same range of $200/month, which in most places in the country yields a bed in a group home, leaving about $37 for incidentals.

Amy K. Glasmeier, Poverty in America, February 26, 2007.
www.povertyinamerica.psu.edu.

"Just as a sinkhole causes everything above it to collapse downward, families and individuals in the middle and upper classes appear to be migrating to lower-income tiers that bring them closer to the poverty threshold," Woolf wrote in the study.

Before Hurricane Katrina, Rene Winn of Biloxi, Miss., earned $28,000 a year as an administrator for the Boys and Girls Club. But for 11 months in 2006, she couldn't find steady work and wouldn't take a fast-food job. As her opportunities dwindled, Winn's frustration grew.

"Some days I feel like the world is mine and I can create my own destiny," she said. "Other days I feel a desperate feeling. Like I gotta' hurry up. Like my career is at a stop. Like I'm getting nowhere fast. And that's not me because I've always been a positive person."

After relocating to New Jersey for 10 months after the storm, Winn returned to Biloxi in September because of medical and emotional problems with her son. She and her two youngest children moved into her sister's home along with her mother, who has Alzheimer's. With her sister, brother-in-law and their two children, eight people now share a three-bedroom home.

Winn said she recently took a job as a technician at the state health department. The hourly job pays $16,120 a year. That's enough to bring her out of severe poverty and just $122 shy of the $16,242 needed for a single mother with two children to escape poverty altogether under current federal guidelines.

Winn eventually wants to transfer to a higher-paying job, but she's thankful for her current position.

"I'm very independent and used to taking care of my own, so I don't like the fact that I have to depend on the state. I want to be able to do it myself."

The Census Bureau's Survey of Income and Program Participation shows that, in a given month, only 10 percent of severely poor Americans received Temporary Assistance for Needy Families in 2003—the latest year available—and that only 36 percent received food stamps.

Many could have exhausted their eligibility for welfare or decided that the new program requirements were too onerous. But the low participation rates are troubling because the worst byproducts of poverty, such as higher crime and violence rates and poor health, nutrition and educational outcomes, are worse for those in deep poverty.

Over the last two decades, America has had the highest or near-highest poverty rates for children, individual adults and families among 31 developed countries, according to the Luxembourg Income Study, a 23-year project that compares poverty and income data from 31 industrial nations.

"It's shameful," said Timothy Smeeding, the former director of the study and the current head of the Center for Policy Research at Syracuse University. "We've been the worst performer every year since we've been doing this study."

With the exception of Mexico and Russia, the U.S. devotes the smallest portion of its gross domestic product to federal anti-poverty programs, and those programs are among the least effective at reducing poverty, the study found. Again, only Russia and Mexico do worse jobs.

One in three Americans will experience a full year of extreme poverty at some point in his or her adult life, according to long-term research by Mark Rank, a professor of social welfare at the Washington University in St. Louis.

An estimated 58 percent of Americans between the ages of 20 and 75 will spend at least a year in poverty, Rank said. Two of three will use a public assistance program between ages 20 and 65, and 40 percent will do so for five years or more.

These estimates apply only to non-immigrants. If illegal immigrants were factored in, the numbers would be worse, Rank said.

"It would appear that for most Americans the question is no longer if, but rather when, they will experience poverty. In short, poverty has become a routine and unfortunate part of the American life course," Rank wrote in a recent study. "Whether these patterns will continue throughout the first decade of 2000 and beyond is difficult to say . . . but there is little reason to think that this trend will reverse itself any time soon."

'Something Real and Troubling'

Most researchers and economists say federal poverty estimates are a poor tool to gauge the complexity of poverty. The numbers don't factor in assistance from government anti-poverty programs, such as food stamps, housing subsidies and the Earned Income Tax Credit, all of which increase incomes and help pull people out of poverty.

But federal poverty measures also exclude work-related expenses and necessities such as day care, transportation, housing and health care costs, which eat up large portions of disposable income, particularly for low-income families.

Alternative poverty measures that account for these shortcomings typically inflate or deflate official poverty statistics. But many of those alternative measures show the same kind of long-term trends as the official poverty data.

Robert Rector, a senior researcher with the Heritage Foundation, a conservative think tank, questioned the growth of severe poverty, saying that census data become less accurate farther down the income ladder. He said many poor people, particularly single mothers with boyfriends, underreport their income by not including cash gifts and loans. Rector said he's seen no data that suggest increasing deprivation among the very poor.

Arloc Sherman of the liberal Center on Budget and Policy Priorities argues that the growing number of severely poor is an indisputable fact.

"When we check against more complete government survey data and administrative records from the benefit programs themselves, they confirm that this trend is real," Sherman said. He added that even among the poor, severely poor people have a much tougher time paying their bills. "That's another sign to me that we're seeing something real and troubling," Sherman said.

> "[Since 1979] the average after-tax in-
> come of the top one percent of the
> population nearly tripled.... The av-
> erage after-tax income of the poorest
> fifth ... rose just 6 percent."

The Gap Between Rich and Poor Is Widening

Arloc Sherman and Aviva Aron-Dine

In the following viewpoint, welfare reform expert Arloc Sherman and federal fiscal policy analyst Aviva Aron-Dine of the Center on Budget and Policy Priorities, a Washington, DC-based non-partisan research organization, present evidence that the so-called income gap—the income difference between the richest and the poorest Americans—is growing year by year: Wealth is heavily concentrated in the top 1 percent of the U.S. population, and the income of this richest group is growing much faster than the income of the middle and lower classes. Sherman and Aron-Dine cite federal tax cuts that have disproportionately benefited the rich as the main reason for the trend, and warn that income inequality will become even more skewed as the most recent tax cuts are phased in.

Arloc Sherman and Aviva Aron-Dine, "New CBO Data Show Income Inequality Continues to Widen," Center on Budget and Policy Priorities, January 23, 2007. Reproduced
by permission.

As you read, consider the following questions:

1. According to the authors, in 2004 what was the average after-tax income of the poorest fifth of the population?

2. What percentage of the national income do the authors claim is concentrated in the top 1 percent of the population?

3. In 2006, how much on average (in dollars) did households in the bottom fifth of the income spectrum receive in tax cuts, according to Sherman and Aron-Dine?

The Congressional Budget Office [CBO] recently released extensive data on household incomes for 2004. CBO issues the most comprehensive and authoritative data available on the levels of and changes in incomes and taxes for different income groups, capturing trends at the very top of the income scale that are not shown in Census data.

The new CBO data document that income inequality continued to widen in 2004. The average *after-tax* income of the richest one percent of households rose from $722,000 in 2003 to $868,000 in 2004, after adjusting for inflation, a one-year increase of nearly $146,000, or 20 percent. This increase was the largest increase in 15 years, measured both in percentage terms and in real dollars.

In contrast, the income of the middle fifth of the population rose $1,700, or 3.6 percent, to $48,400 in 2004. The income of the bottom fifth rose a scant $200 (or 1.4 percent) to $14,700.

A Twenty-Five-Year Trend

The new data also highlight the degree to which income gains over the past quarter-century have become increasingly concentrated at the top of the income scale. Since 1979—the first year for which the CBO data are available—income gains among high-income households have dwarfed those of middle- and low-income households. Over this 25-year period:

- The average after-tax income of the top one percent of the population nearly tripled, rising from $314,000 to nearly $868,000—for a total increase of $554,000, or 176 percent. (Figures throughout this paper were adjusted by CBO for inflation and are presented in 2004 dollars.)

- By contrast, the average after-tax income of the middle fifth of the population rose a relatively modest 21 percent, or $8,500, reaching $48,400 in 2004.

- The average after-tax income of the poorest fifth of the population rose just 6 percent, or $800, over the past 25 years, reaching $14,700 in 2004.

Because incomes grew much faster among the most affluent, this group's share of the total national income also increased.

- The top one percent of the population received 14.0 percent of the national after-tax income in 2004, nearly double its 7.5 percent share in 1979. (Each percentage point of after-tax income is equivalent to $71 billion in 2004 dollars.)

- In contrast, the middle fifth of the population, which has 20 times more people in it, received 15.0 percent of the national after-tax income in 2004, down from 16.5 percent in 1979. The bottom fifth received 4.9 percent of the income in 2004, down from 6.8 percent in 1979.

Income is now more concentrated at the top of the income spectrum than in all but two years since the mid-1930s. This conclusion is reached by examining the CBO data in conjunction with data from a ground-breaking historical analysis of pre-tax income distribution trends published in a leading economics journal. When viewed together, the studies indicate that the top one percent of households now receive a larger share of the national pre-tax income than at any time since 1937, except for the years 1999 and 2000.

Income Gaps Widened in 2004

The CBO data show that gaps in income inequality widened significantly between 2003 and 2004. The share of after-tax income going to the top one percent rose from 12.2 percent in 2003 to 14.0 percent in 2004, an increase of 1.8 percentage points. As noted above, this amounts to $146,000 per household in the top one percent, equivalent to an additional $128 billion in income for the top one percent as a whole. This is the largest one-year increase in the share of income going to the top one percent in 15 years. The CBO data go back to 1979.

The growing concentration of income at the top continues a long-term trend. Income concentration grew steadily during the latter half of the 1990s, and peaked in 2000, a year that the stock market hit a record high. From 2000 to 2002, income became less concentrated at the very top, partially due to the drop in the stock market; after-tax incomes fell from 2000 to 2002 for most income groups, but declined the most for the top one percent. In 2003 and 2004, however, the long-term trend toward growing income inequality returned.

Tax Policies Exacerbating Income Gaps

The CBO data also indicate that the growth in income disparities since 1979 largely reflects changes in *before*-tax income. That is, most of the divergence in income patterns among various income groups reflects diverging outcomes in the income that they received before taking changes in federal tax policies into account. Nonetheless, changes in federal taxes have had some influence over these patterns.

The direction in which the tax system influences inequality depends on the time period examined. Changes in federal tax policies exacerbated the growth in income disparities dur-

American Dream Receding for Many

Children from lower-income families have only a 1 percent chance of reaching the top 5 percent of the income distribution, versus children of wealthier families who have about a 22 percent chance. Consequently, more families below the $25,000 income threshold or in deep poverty mean fewer children will have a shot at the American Dream.

The steady rise in income inequality only exacerbates this challenge of upward economic mobility. . . . Growing income inequality makes economic mobility more difficult because as the "rungs on the ladder" get further and further apart, it becomes increasingly difficult for families to climb up. In other words, the challenge that low-income and middle class families face in trying to move up the economic ladder is greater when they have to travel a farther distance to get there.

Derek Douglas and Almas Sayeed,
Center for Economic Progress,
September 1, 2006.

ing the 1980s, when taxes were cut sharply for high-income individuals, but slowed the growth in income disparities during the 1990s, when tax rates for high-income households were raised and the Earned Income Tax Credit for low- and moderate-income working families was substantially expanded.

Legislation enacted since 2001 has provided taxpayers with about $1 trillion in tax cuts over the past six years. These large tax reductions have made the distribution of after-tax income more unequal. Because high-income households received by far the largest tax cuts, the tax cuts have increased the concentration of income at the top of the spectrum.

The CBO data provide additional evidence that the recent tax cuts have contributed to the widening income gaps. CBO provides data on *effective* federal income tax rates—that is, on the share of income that is paid in income taxes—for different groups of households. While all groups of households have seen declines in their effective federal income-tax rates since 2000, the declines have been much larger for the highest income taxpayers. For example, between 2000 and 2004, households in the top one percent of the income spectrum saw a drop in their effective federal income-tax rate of about 4.6 percentage points, more than twice the drop for households in the middle quintile (2.1 percentage points). This decline in the effective rate translated into an average income tax reduction of almost $58,000 for people in the top one percent, relative to what these households would have paid if their effective tax rate had remained unchanged.

A Direct Result of Tax Cuts

These data do not provide a direct measure of the impact of tax policy changes because they reflect the impact not only of legislative changes but also of changes in household incomes and other factors that influence tax rates. Direct estimates by the Urban Institute–Brookings Institution Tax Policy Center that consider *only* the impact of the recent tax policy changes provide definitive evidence that the recent-tax cuts have widened income inequality. The Tax Policy Center finds that as a result of the tax cuts enacted since 2001:

- In 2006, households in the bottom fifth of the income spectrum received tax cuts (averaging $20) that raised their after-tax incomes by an average of 0.3 percent.

- Households in the middle fifth of the income spectrum received tax cuts (averaging $740) that raised their after-tax incomes an average of 2.5 percent.

- But the top one percent of households received tax cuts in 2006 (averaging $44,200) that increased their after-tax income by an average of 5.4 percent.

- Households with incomes exceeding $1 million received an average tax cut of $118,000 in 2006, which represented an increase of 6.0 percent in their after-tax income. That is more than double the percentage increase received by the middle fifth of households.

Finally, some of the tax cuts enacted in 2001 are still being phased in, and the tax cuts still phasing in are heavily tilted to people at the top of the income scale. These include the elimination of the tax on the nation's largest estates and two income-tax cuts that started to take effect on January 1, 2006 and will go almost exclusively to high-income households. As a result, the tax cuts ultimately will be even more skewed toward high-income households, and will increase income inequality to a still larger degree, than was the case in 2006.

"There is surprisingly little U.S. evidence of any significant and sustained increase in inequality of income, wealth, wages, or consumption since the late 1980s."

The Gap Between Rich and Poor Is Not Widening

Alan Reynolds

Economist Alan Reynolds is a senior fellow at the Cato Institute, a libertarian think tank in Washington, DC, and the author of Income and Wealth. *In the following viewpoint, Reynolds disputes the claim that the gap between the richest and poorest segments of the U.S. population has grown in recent years and is indeed accelerating. On the contrary, Reynolds maintains, the figures used to make this claim—based on personal income tax returns—are invalid. It only* looks *like the rich have gotten much richer, for example, because tax policies have changed and wealthy people are reporting as personal income what used to be reported as corporate income. Similarly, middle-class taxpayers are reporting* less *income only because more of their income is nontaxable in the form of various retirement and savings plans.*

Alan Reynolds, "Has U.S. Iuncome Inequality Really Increased?" *Policy Analysis*, January 8, 2007, pp. 2–4, 6–9, 18–19, 21–22. Copyright © 2007 Cato Institute. All rights reserved. Reproduced by permission.

And it only looks *like the poorest Americans' income has stagnated because the substantial Social Security income and government benefits they receive are not counted.*

As you read, consider the following questions:
1. What popular income shelters make it look like middle-class and lower-wage earners' incomes have not risen when in fact they *have* risen, according to Reynolds?
2. Why are media reports of a widening income gap that compare "the top 1 percent" of income to the lowest share of income misleading, in Reynolds's opinion?
3. How does the author arrive at the conclusion that the income of the lowest 80 percent of American taxpayers has steadily risen at an accelerating rate since 1982?

M ajor newspapers and magazines repeatedly report that the share of national income received by the top 1 percent in the United States (the roughly 1.3 million tax returns with the highest reported incomes in the United States) has increased enormously and continuously since the 1970s. Of the many difficult statistics used to influence public perception and policy, this one is surely the most often repeated and the least often understood. . . .

Income equality studies that are based on data reported on federal tax returns can be highly misleading. [Several] major factors have seriously distorted measurements of income inequality in recent decades. The following sections examine those factors and discuss the extent to which they have affected published inequality data.

Tax Cuts and Income Conversion

The *Economist* has depicted the apparent rise in the top 1 percent's share as a "truly continuous trend." But that is not what the data actually show. Instead, the reported income share of the top 1 percent has changed sharply in periods when tax rules have changed. The 2001 paper by [Thomas] Piketty and [Emmanuel] Saez clearly explained that, "a significant part of the gain [in top income shares] is concentrated in two years, 1987 and 1988, just after the Tax Reform Act of 1986."

The top 1 percent's share jumped from 9.1 percent in 1985 and 1986, when the top tax rate was 50 percent, to 13.2 percent in 1988 when the top tax rate dropped to 28 percent. That was not a sudden two-year spurt in inequality. It was a sudden increase in the amount of high income reported on individual income tax returns rather than being concealed, deferred, or reported on *corporate* income tax returns. Dramatic changes in tax laws have changed the way that income has been reported on tax returns over time.

As discussed below, many studies of the elasticity (responsiveness) of reported income to changes in marginal tax rates by Emmanuel Saez and others show that when the highest tax rates are reduced, the amount of income reported on tax returns rises. The two-year spurt in income reported by the top 1 percent is therefore exactly what economists would have expected to happen after the top tax rate on income was cut from 50 percent in 1986, to 37.5 percent in 1987, and to 28 percent in 1988. . . .

When individual tax rates were reduced after the 1981 tax act and again after the 1986 tax act, it provided a strong incentive to shift from reporting business income on corporate returns to individual returns by filing as S-corporations, limited liability companies (LLCs), partnerships, or proprietorships. In all these cases, business profits flow through to individual returns rather than being taxed at the corporate level on corporate tax returns.

One result is that those attempting to measure incomes by what has been reported on individual tax returns may erroneously view these large increases in income at the top as real changes in American's incomes. Instead, they were simply the result of a bookkeeping change in the way business incomes were reported. Switching income from corporate returns to individual returns did not make the rich any richer—it simply made more of their income show up as "individual income" in the CBO [Congressional Budget Office] and Piketty-Saez estimates. . . .

This bookkeeping change related to where businesses report their income is only one factor of many that distorts often-cited measures of income inequality. But this factor alone is reason enough to make it illegitimate to use individual income tax data to compare shares of income over time, particularly before and after the monumental tax law changes of 1981 and 1986.

Increasingly Invisible Investment Income

A variety of factors have served to depress the denominator of the ratio of top incomes to total incomes in recent decades. If large amounts of income for those near the bottom and in the middle are not reported on tax returns, it means that the income share of those at the top is being exaggerated. A very important factor in this regard is that prior to the 1980s nearly all income from investments (dividends, interest, and capital gains) was reported on individual tax returns. But in recent years, an increasingly large share of middle-income investment returns have been sheltered inside tax-favored accounts, such as 401(k)s, Individual Retirement Arrangements (IRAs), and 529 college savings plans. Investment income accruing in tax-favored savings plans is not recorded on income tax returns. . . .

By contrast, the bulk of investment income of those in the top 1 percent is still reported on tax returns, because most of it is taxable and not in the various tax-favored accounts such as IRAs and 401(k)s. . . .

Before a variety of tax-favored savings plans became commonplace, virtually every dollar of investment income from the savings of middle-income taxpayers was reported as taxable income, and it was therefore counted as income in studies that use tax returns to estimate income distribution in the 1970s. Today, by contrast, most investment returns from the saving of middle-income taxpayers are rarely or never taxed. This makes it singularly inappropriate to use tax data to compare income shares before and after the explosion of tax-deferred accounts. Doing so makes it appear as though middle-income investors had a far larger share of capital gains, dividends, and interest income in the 1970s than they did in the 1990s, simply because those investments used to be fully taxable and now are not. The actual increase of incomes among middle-income households since the 1970s is therefore greatly understated in tax data because an increasingly huge portion of their investment income is no longer reported on tax returns. . . .

Top 1 Percent of What?

Media reports about the supposed rise in the income share at the top, including references to the Piketty-Saez studies, never bother to ask the most basic question of all: the top 1 percent of *what?*

Most people assume that the "top 1 percent" and other income shares refer to the top percentiles of *household* or *family* income. *New York Times* columnist Paul Krugman wrote: "According to Piketty and Saez . . . in 1998 the top 0.01 percent received more than 3 percent of all income. That meant that the 13,000 richest families in America had almost as much income as the 20 million poorest households." Yet the Piketty-Saez figures do not refer to households nor families (much less both)—they refer to "tax units," which can be much different.

Piketty and Saez point out that "average household income is about 28 percent higher than average tax unit income." In some cases the differences are much larger than

The Income Gap Between Whites and Blacks Is Shrinking

In 1984, the average white person in America made $6,526 more per year than the average black person. Nearly 20 years later, in 2002, the average white person made $10,902 more per year than the average black person. On the surface, it might appear as though the black/white income gap is worsening, but things are not always as they appear. In fact, the gap is actually shrinking at a steady pace. The $6,526 in 1984 represented a 35% gap between Whites and Blacks, while the $10,902 in 2002 represented a 27% gap. The income gap is shrinking at a pace of about half a percent per year, and using that model, the gap should completely close by the year 2062.

Jimmy Smith, July 29, 2007.
http://jimmysmithblog.blogspot.com.

that. Two unmarried working people living together constitute one household but two tax units; their household income could be twice as large as their income per tax unit. Or consider that children with investment income above $750 are required to file tax returns, with the result that they show up as extremely poor "tax units" in the Piketty-Saez figures, even though they are unlikely to be living in poor families.

Pointing to the Piketty-Saez data, the preceding remark by Paul Krugman claimed the 13,000 richest "families" received "more than 3 percent of all income." But these are not "families," they are tax units. Also note that Piketty and Saez do not measure "all income." The authors do not include benefit payments from Social Security, Temporary Assistance for Needy Families, the Earned Income Tax Credit, Supplemental Security Income, or other government programs. Since not all income is counted, such figures cannot possibly tell us what share of all income was received by those at the top.

In 1970, wages and salaries accounted for 65.8 percent of personal income, while transfer payments accounted for just 8.5 percent. In 2005, wages and salaries accounted for 55.3 percent of personal income, while transfers accounted for 14.5 percent. Because transfer payments have represented a rising share of total income, ignoring them makes the top 1 percents share appear to increase because a growing fraction of other people's income is not counted. Yet there is no logical reason to arbitrarily exclude such benefits as Social Security from measured income, while including comparable benefits from private retirement plans.

The top 1 percent's share of income is a *ratio*—the top 1 percent's income is the numerator, and that plus everyone else's income is the denominator. Excluding transfer payments from the denominator makes the top 1 percent's share appear larger than it really is, but it also makes the top 1 percent's share appear to rise more than it has because transfer payments have accounted for a rising share of actual total income (the denominator). . . .

Income Trends Since the 1970s

The widespread impression that the United States has experienced a large and continuous increase in income inequality since the 1970s is almost entirely dependent on the disingenuous practice of using estimates based on income tax returns to compare the distribution of incomes before and after the dramatic tax changes of 1981 and 1986. If the Piketty and Saez estimates actually demonstrated a continuous and credible upward trend toward greater inequality since the late-1980s, all other estimates of income distribution would have to be wrong—including those of the Census Bureau, the CBO, and the Federal Reserve Board.

In a recent column, Paul Krugman complained about "the amount of time that inequality's apologists spend attacking a claim nobody is making: that there has been a clear long-term decline in middle-class living standards." Yet, in a 2004 column Krugman said, "according to estimates by the economists Thomas Piketty and Emmanuel Saez—confirmed by data from the CBO—between 1973 and 2000 the average real income of the bottom 90 percent of American taxpayers actually fell by 7 percent."

For Krugman to assert that there was a 7 percent drop in real income for 90 percent of taxpayers over 27 years certainly sounds like a "clear long-term decline in middle-class living standards." To question such claims requires no straw man. On the contrary, Krugman's astonishingly incorrect assertion provided an excellent example of how remarkably uncritical even professional economists have become toward the Piketty-Saez estimates.

Piketty and Saez recently acknowledged that, "our long-run series are generally confined to top income and wealth shares and contain little information about bottom segments of the distribution." Yet one of their figures from their 2001 paper encouraged the exact opposite impression. The figure *appeared* to show 27 years of real income stagnation (not decline) for the bottom *99 percent* of taxpayers rather than Krugman's bottom 90 percent. In a key footnote to that graph, however, they explain that "from 1973 to 2000, the average income of the bottom 99 percent would have grown by about 40 percent in real terms instead of stagnating if we had included all transfers (+7% effect), used the CPI-U-RS [consumer price index research series using current methods] (+13% effect), and especially defined income per capita (20% effect)." That 40 percent increase in per capita real income for the bottom 99 percent makes it quite impossible that income of the bottom 90 percent of American taxpayers "actually fell by 7 percent," as Krugman wrote.

CBO's estimates began in 1979, not 1973, and they certainly do not "confirm" what Piketty and Saez deny (in the footnote). Between 1979 and 2000, the CBO estimates indicate that the average real income of the bottom 80 percent of American taxpayers *rose* by 12 percent before taxes and by 15 percent after taxes. Real after-tax income of the middle quintile rose from $38,900 in 1979 (in 2003 dollars) to $44,700 in 2000, according to the CBO.

Census Bureau estimates of mean household income among the bottom four quintiles rose from $32,786 in 1973 (in 2005 dollars) to $40,640 in 2000. That is, Census estimates show a 24 percent real increase for the bottom 80 percent—with all of that gain occurring since 1982. In fact, the Census estimates show an *accelerating pace* of gains among the bottom 80 percent, with real income in that group rising 7.6 percent from 1970 to 1980, 9.6 percent from 1980 to 1990, and 12.4 percent from 1990 to 2000.

Aside from the Piketty-Saez comparisons of top income shares before and after the Tax Reform Act of 1986, there is surprisingly little U.S. evidence of any significant and sustained increase in inequality of income, wealth, wages, or consumption since the late 1980s. . . .

In sum, studies of changes in income distribution based on tax return data provide distorted and misleading comparisons of U.S. income shares because of dramatic changes in tax laws in recent decades. Aside from changes in taxpayer reporting due to changes in the tax laws, there is no clear evidence of a significant and sustained increase in the inequality of U.S. incomes, wages, consumption, or wealth since the late 1980s.

Periodical Bibliography

The following articles have been selected to supplement the diverse views presented in this chapter.

Douglas J. Besharov	"Measuring Poverty in America," American Enterprise Institute, August 1, 2007. www.aei.org/publications/pubID.26594/pub_detail.asp.
Neil deMause	and Steve Rendall, "The Poor Will Always Be with Us—Just Not on the TV News," Fairness & Accuracy In Reporting *Extra*, September/October 2007. www.fair.org/index.php?page=3172.
David R. Francis	"The War on Poverty Is Winnable," *Christian Science Monitor*, April 2, 2007.
Harry Holzer et al.	"The Economic Costs of Poverty in the United States," *Center for American Progress*, January 24, 2007.
Bruce Katz	"United States Conference of Mayors Task Force on Work, Poverty, and Opportunity Presentation," Metropolitan Policy Program, Brookings Institution, June 2, 2006. www.brookings.edu/speeches/2006/0602metropolitanpolicy_katz.aspx.
Eyal Press	"The New Suburban Poverty," *Nation*, April 23, 2007.
U.S. Government Accountability Office	"Poverty in America: Highlights," GAO-07-344, January 2007. www.gao.gov/new.items/d07344.pdf.
Yolanda Woodlee	"One-Third of Children in Poverty, Report Says," *Washington Post*, January 18, 2008.
Patricia Zapor	"U.S. Welfare 10 Years Later: Some Success, but Poverty Growing Again," *Catholic Online*, August 2, 2006. www.catholic.org/national/national_story.php?id=20746.

CHAPTER 2

What Causes Poverty in America?

Chapter Preface

Theories of the causes of poverty generally fall into one of two categories. The first comprises what are usually called individual causes, which explain poverty in terms of poor people's circumstances or characteristics: education, skills, intelligence, health, age. The second category includes so-called generic theories of poverty, which argue that broad economic trends and historical forces beyond individual control cause poverty: lack of employment opportunity, welfare or immigration policy, racial or class discrimination. There is a third category—acute causes such as warfare, agricultural cycles, and natural disasters—but because these factors are historically (and by definition) short-term, they take a backseat in the debate over the causes of poverty in the United States and what to do about it.

The third category is likely to get a lot more attention, however, as the adverse impacts of climate change, and the links between global warming and poverty in developed as well as developing countries, become clearer. In the United States, climate change may not mean widespread famine or impoverishment to the degree predicted in Africa and Asia, but everywhere global warming exacerbates existing vulnerabilities and poses a threat to the people least equipped to adapt to it.

Predicted effects of global warming in the United States include shifts in precipitation patterns resulting in drought, water shortages, and agricultural losses (especially in the Southwest, which some scientists predict will become as arid as the Dust Bowl of the 1930s); flooding and more intense storms (especially in the Southeast); and more intense summer heat waves and winter cold snaps. According to a 2006 National Hispanic Environmental Council publication, these developments will disproportionately affect agricultural workers, the elderly, and people in "older, poor-quality housing less likely to be financially prepared to evacuate or relocate in the event of a natural disaster. Mobile homes are particularly vulnerable." A warmer climate also means "more areas of the U.S. will be hospitable to malaria, St. Louis encephalitis, Lyme disease, and Dengue fever and rodents, carriers of the hanta virus," as well as ozone-smog-related asthma, posing particular risks to the uninsured. As physican and epidemiologist Larry Brilliant stated in 2007, "The poor get sicker and the sick get poorer, and as the climate crisis deepens, without intervention, there will be many more sick, and many more poor."

This view is offset by researchers who predict that global warming will actually increase food production in many parts of the United States, and by environmental activists who see the effort to reduce the impact of climate change as an opportunity to create as many as 500,000 "green-collar jobs" in new industries by 2010. California environmentalist Van Jones points to "vocational job[s] in an ecologically responsible trade, for instance: installing solar panels, weatherizing buildings, constructing and maintaining wind farms, materials reuse and recycling, doing organic agriculture, etc." Climate change may soon be at the forefront of the debate over the causes of poverty considered in the viewpoints in this chapter.

> *"The current influx of low-skill immigrants will raise poverty in the U.S. not merely at the present time, but for generations to come."*

Immigration Is Increasing Poverty in the United States

Robert Rector

U.S. immigration policy since the mid-1960s has increased poverty, argues Robert Rector, senior fellow at the conservative Washington, DC, think tank the Heritage Foundation. Rector cites two factors for this trend: an immigration system that "favors kinship ties over skills and education" and lax, inadequate government programs that would stop illegal immigration at the border and prohibit employment of illegal immigrants. The result, he maintains, is an influx of 10.5 million immigrants with "low levels of education, high levels of poverty, and high levels of out-of-wedlock childbearing"—all factors that increase the probability of receiving government services and welfare benefits.

Robert Rector, "Importing Poverty: Immigration and Poverty in the United States," *Heritage Special Report SR-9*, October 25, 2006, pp. 1–5, 28–29. Copyright © 2006 The Heritage Foundation. Reproduced by permission.

As you read, consider the following questions:

1. What percentage of all poor persons in the United States are first-generation immigrants and their families, according to Rector?

2. How much does Rector estimate it will cost American taxpayers to support the 6 million legal immigrants who lack a high school diploma?

3. How does the author counter the argument that high-skill immigrants (a net fiscal plus for American taxpayers) cancel out low-skill immigrants, so no change in immigration policy is necessary?

In 1963, President Lyndon Johnson launched the War on Poverty with the goal of eliminating poverty in the United States. Since that time, the U.S. has spent over $11 trillion on anti-poverty programs, providing cash, food, housing, medical care, and services to the poor and near poor. Today, government provides a generous system of benefits and services to both the working and non-working poor. While government continues its massive efforts to reduce poverty, immigration policy in the U.S. has come to operate in the opposite direction, increasing rather than decreasing poverty. Immigrants with low skill levels have a high probability of both poverty and receipt of welfare benefits and services.

Immigrants Lack Education and Skills

Since the immigration reforms of the 1960s, the U.S. has imported poverty through immigration policies that permitted and encouraged the entry and residence of millions of low-skill immigrants into the nation. Low-skill immigrants tend to be poor and to have children who, in turn, add to America's poverty problem, driving up governmental welfare, social service, and education costs.

Today's immigrants differ greatly from historic immigrant populations. Prior to 1960, immigrants to the U.S. had education levels that were similar to those of the non-immigrant workforce and earned wages that were, on average, higher than those of non-immigrant workers. Since the mid-1960s, however, the education levels of new immigrants have plunged relative to non-immigrants; consequently, the average wages of immigrants are now well below those of the non-immigrant population. Recent immigrants increasingly occupy the low end of the U.S. socio-economic spectrum.

The current influx of poorly educated immigrants is the result of two factors: first, a legal immigration system that favors kinship ties over skills and education; and second, a permissive attitude toward illegal immigration that has led to lax border enforcement and non-enforcement of the laws that prohibit the employment of illegal immigrants. In recent years, these factors have produced an inflow of some ten and a half million immigrants who lack a high school education. In terms of increased poverty and expanded government expenditure, this importation of poorly educated immigrants has had roughly the same effect as the addition of ten and a half million native-born high school drop-outs.

As a result of this dramatic inflow of low-skill immigrants,

- One-third of all immigrants live in families in which the head of the household lacks a high school education; and

- First-generation immigrants and their families, who are one-sixth of the U.S. population, comprise one-fourth of all poor persons in the U.S.

Immigration also plays a large role in child poverty:

- Some 38 percent of immigrant children live in families headed by persons who lack a high school education;

- Minor children of first-generation immigrants comprise 26 percent of poor children in the U.S.; and

- One out of six poor children in the U.S. is the offspring of first-generation immigrant parents who lack a high school diploma.

Poverty Prevalent Among Hispanic Immigrants

Hispanic immigrants (both legal and illegal) comprise half of all first-generation immigrants and their families. Poverty is especially prevalent among this group. Hispanic immigrants have particularly low levels of education; more than half live in families headed by persons who lack a high school diploma. Family formation is also weak among Hispanic immigrants; fully 42 percent of the children of Hispanic immigrants are born out of wedlock. Hispanic immigrants thus make up a disproportionate share of the nation's poor:

1. First-generation Hispanic immigrants and their families now comprise 9 percent of the U.S. population but 17 percent of all poor persons in the U.S.; and

2. Children in Hispanic immigrant families now comprise 11.7 percent of all children in the U.S. but 22 percent of all poor children in the U.S.

Massive low-skill immigration works to counteract government anti-poverty efforts. While government works to reduce the number of poor persons, low-skill immigration pushes the poverty numbers up. In addition, low-skill immigration siphons off government anti-poverty funding and makes government efforts to shrink poverty less effective.

Low-skill immigrants pay little in taxes and receive high levels of government benefits and services. The National Academy of Sciences has estimated that each immigrant without a high school degree will cost U.S. taxpayers, on average, $89,000 over the course of his or her lifetime. This is a net cost above the value of any taxes the immigrant will pay and does not include the cost of educating the immigrant's children, which U.S. taxpayers would also heavily subsidize.

Poor Immigrants Cost Taxpayers

In this way, the roughly six million legal immigrants without a high school diploma will impose a net cost of around a half-trillion dollars on U.S. taxpayers over their lifetimes. The roughly five million illegal immigrants without a high school diploma will cost taxpayers somewhat less because illegal immigrants are eligible for fewer government benefits. However, if these illegal immigrants were granted amnesty and citizenship, as proposed by the [George W.] Bush Administration and legislated in a [May 2006] Senate-passed immigration bill (S. 2611), they could cost taxpayers an additional half-trillion dollars. In total, all immigrants without a high school education could impose a net cost on U.S. taxpayers of around one trillion dollars or more. If the cost of educating the immigrants' children is included, that figure could reach two trillion dollars.

The poverty and other problems associated with mass low-skill immigration would be of less concern if they could be expected to quickly vanish in the next generation. Unfortunately, the evidence indicates that this will not occur. For example, the low levels of education, high levels of poverty, and high levels of out-of-wedlock childbearing found among Hispanic immigrants since 1970 persist among native-born Hispanics in the U.S. to a considerable degree.

These data indicate that the current influx of low-skill immigrants will raise poverty in the U.S. not merely at the present time, but for generations to come. Current low-skill immigrants will raise both the absolute number of poor persons and the poverty rate in the U.S. for the foreseeable future. The greater the inflow of low-skill immigrants, the greater the long-term increase in poverty will be. . . .

Defining the Immigrant Population

One basic issue in measuring immigrant poverty relates to the treatment of minor children born to immigrant parents in the

U.S. For example, consider the case of a woman who comes to the U.S. from a foreign country and gives birth to a child in the U.S. without being married. Because the child was born on U.S. soil, he or she is automatically a U.S. citizen. Further, assume that the mother and the child live together and are poor.

The mother and child both add to the ranks of poor persons in the U.S. Conceivably, one might count the mother's poverty as part of immigrant poverty and the child's poverty as part of non-immigrant poverty. In reality, the expansion of U.S. poverty is, in both cases, a consequence of the mother's immigration to the U.S. The number of poor persons would be two fewer if the immigration had not occurred. Thus, it seems reasonable to count both poor immigrants and poor minor children born in the U.S. to immigrant parents as components of immigrant poverty. . . .

Overall, 49.3 million first-generation immigrants and their family members lived in the U.S. in 2004; some 13.9 million were children. First-generation immigrants and their family members comprised 16.9 percent of the population. The non-immigrant population numbered 241.8 million, or 83.1 percent of the population. Of these, 59.7 million were children.

Among first-generation immigrants and their families living in the U.S. in 2004, Hispanics and Asians predominated. Half of first-generation immigrants and family members lived in Hispanic-headed households, and 20 percent lived in Asian-headed households. Some 21 percent lived in households with white non-Hispanic heads, and 8 percent lived in households headed by blacks. . . .

A More Selective Immigration Policy

Immigrants and their families now comprise one out of four poor Americans. Poor immigrants pay little in taxes and consume large levels of government services including medical care, welfare, and public education. The increase in poverty

Education Suffers for Impoverished Latino Children

While California voters voted down a proposition that would have provided free preschool to 4-year-olds earlier this year [2006], the state is set to invest hundreds of millions of dollars to provide early education to poor children, the group likely to profit most from high quality programs.

In order to deliver on the promise of pre-K, states will need to aggressively reach out to the fastest-growing part of our population: Latino children. Only 40 percent of Latino 3- to 5-year-olds attend preschool, compared with approximately 60 percent of both African-American and white children. Ironically, Latinos are particularly in need of early intervention: They often live in poverty, their parents generally have low levels of education, and in recently arrived immigrant families, children's exposure to English can be minimal.

Publicity is an integral part of raising awareness about preschool in Latino communities. A March 2006 poll commissioned by the advocacy group PreK Now found that over half of Latinos felt that early education was out of their reach because they either weren't aware of existing programs or figured they couldn't afford them even if they did know where to look.

Alexandra Starr,
"Free Preschool Will Help Latinos and US,"
Christian Science Monitor, *August 21, 2006.*
Copyright © 2006 Christian Science Monitor.
Reproduced by permission of the author.

due to immigration can impose costs well beyond the immediate cost of current welfare benefits for immigrants. By magnifying the public perception of poverty, immigration can create political leverage for new anti-poverty programs. Immigration-induced poverty can easily have spillover effects resulting in new government entitlements for all poor Americans.

The U.S. offers enormous economic opportunities and societal benefits. Hundreds of millions more people would immigrate to the U.S. if they had the opportunity. Given this context, the U.S. must be selective in its immigration policy. Policymakers must ensure that the interaction of welfare and immigration does not expand the welfare-dependent population, thereby hindering rather than helping immigrants and imposing large costs on American society.

U.S. immigration policy should encourage high-skill immigration and strictly limit low-skill immigration. In general, government policy should limit immigration to those who will be net fiscal contributors, avoiding those who will increase poverty and impose new costs on overburdened U.S. taxpayers.

It is sometimes argued that since higher-skill immigrants are a net fiscal plus for the U.S. taxpayers while low-skill immigrants are a net loss, the two cancel each other out and therefore no problem exists. This is like a stock broker advising a client to buy two stocks, one which will make money and another that will lose money. Obviously, it would be better to purchase only the stock that will be profitable and avoid the money losing stock entirely. Similarly, low-skill immigrants increase poverty in the U.S. and impose a burden on taxpayers that should be avoided.

Current legislative proposals that would grant amnesty to illegal immigrants and increase future low-skill immigration would represent the largest expansion of the welfare state in 30 years. Such proposals would increase poverty in the U.S. in the short and long term and dramatically increase the burden on U.S. taxpayers.

| "Over the 1994–2000 period, poverty rates fell much more quickly for immigrants than for natives."

Immigration Is Not Increasing Poverty in the United States

Jeff Chapman and Jared Bernstein

Jeff Chapman is a policy analyst and Jared Bernstein an economist at the Economic Policy Institute in Washington, DC, a nonprofit think tank that represents the interests of low- and middle-income workers in the debate over economic policy. In the following viewpoint, Chapman and Bernstein disagree with claims that the growing immigrant share of the U.S. population accounts for a flat or rising poverty rate. Indeed, they argue, poverty rates have fallen faster for immigrants than for natives. The authors connect the poverty rate more closely to fundamentally economic factors, such as inequality and unemployment, which "hurt the economic prospects of all low-wage workers, not just immigrants."

As you read, consider the following questions:

1. What important distinction do Chapman and Bernstein make between immigrant share and immigrant income?

Jeff Chapman and Jared Bernstein, "Immigration and Poverty: How Are They Linked?" *Monthly Labor Review*, April 2003, pp. 10–15. Reproduced by permission.

2. How much did the median income of immigrant families increase compared with the median income of native families from 1994 to 2000, according to the authors?

3. Why do the authors point to California and New York as proof that immigration is not the primary cause of rising poverty rates?

Data from the 2000 census show that the Nation's poverty rate fell less than 1 percentage point, from 13.1 percent to 12.4 percent, between 1989 and 1999. In some States, including California and New York, the poverty rate was higher in 1999 than in 1989. In addition, some areas of the country posted only small increases in real median family income, even given the strong economy of the latter 1990s. For example, census data reveal that median annual family income in New York grew only $113 (0.2 percent) in real terms over the decade.

Immigrant Share vs. Immigrant Income

Media coverage has attributed the findings regarding poverty chiefly to the effects of a growing immigrant population composed of many low-income families. The idea is that, because the immigrant share of the population increased from 1989 to 1999, and because immigrants' incomes are, on average, lower than natives', overall income growth was subject to a downward pressure over the decade a phenomenon referred to in this article as the share effect. The question, however, is whether the share effect does in fact implicate immigration as the sole, or even the most important, factor behind the census figures. Without more evidence, the role of immigration in what are essentially flat poverty statistics remains open.

The needed evidence is at least twofold. First, the magnitude of the share effect must be quantified, that is, how much did the increase in the share of the immigrant population lower real income or raise the poverty rate? Second, the impact of the share effect can be offset by trends in immigrants' own income and poverty status, here in called the income effect. Thus, analysts need to quantify this effect as well, to learn whether and by how much it contributed to changes in real income or the poverty rate.

In a period such as the 1990s, when both the population share and the incomes of immigrants rose, the question of immigration's impact can be viewed as the outcome of a race between the share and income effects. That is, did immigrants' income improve fast enough to offset the downward pressure exerted by their increased share in the population? Without quantifying these two countervailing effects, researchers have little useful authoritative information to bring to the discussion. This article shows that, over the 1994–2000 period, immigrants' rising incomes offset the negative impact of their rising shares. . . .

The available data introduce a note of caution regarding any interpretation of the census results that depends heavily on increased immigration. To bring out the caution required of any such interpretation, [this viewpoint] examines both national data and data from New York and California—two States in which one might expect immigration to play a large role in the determination of the poverty rate. These States are important to consider because (1) more than 1 in 4 New Yorkers and 1 in 3 Californians are immigrants and (2) both States had poverty rates that were higher in 1999 than in 1989, according to Census 2000 data.

An analysis of the currently available data brings out the following facts:

- Over the 1994–2000 period, poverty rates fell much more quickly for immigrants than for natives. For example, the national poverty rates of recent immigrants (those here for 10 or fewer years) fell about 4 times as fast as that of natives (11.6 percentage points, compared with 2.9 points); the rate for all immigrants fell 2.7 times as fast as that of U.S natives.

- Immigrant families also experienced greater increases than U.S. natives did in real median family incomes from 1994 to 2000. After adjustment for inflation, the median family incomes of immigrants rose 26.3 percent during the period, while the median family incomes of native U.S. families grew half that fast. For recent immigrants, the growth in real median family income was an even greater 40.5 percent.

- These gains in immigrant income over the 1994–2000 period were substantial enough to offset the negative impact of the share effect.

- A preliminary analysis of the census figures for California and New York from 1989 to 1999 indicated that the increase in immigration added about 1 percentage point to the growth in poverty over the decade. Absent this effect, poverty would have been unchanged in California and would have risen slightly in New York.

- Immigration did not play as large a role as other more fundamentally economic factors, such as inequality and unemployment, in keeping the poverty rate relatively flat. These factors hurt the economic prospects of all low-wage workers, not just immigrants.

Poverty Rates and Median Family Income

Based on March 2003 Current Population Survey (cps) data, immigrants are much more likely to live in poverty than are natives. . . .

Indeed, the poverty rate of recent immigrants is more than twice that of U.S. natives. Because of this, at any point in time, the poverty rate would most certainly be lower in the absence of immigration. Also, increasing the immigrant share will raise the poverty rate. However, as noted, this share effect, as well as the offsetting income effect (the impact of faster income growth among immigrants), that occurred over the 1989–99 period needs to be quantified. . . .

The national poverty rates of recent immigrants fell about 4 times as fast as they did for U.S. natives from 1994 to 2000; the rates for all immigrants fell 2.7 times as fast as those of U.S. natives during the same period. . . . Again based on March CPSdata, the poverty rates of immigrants living in New York and California fell even further than did the poverty rates of U.S. natives:

From 1994 to 2000, the poverty rates of recent immigrants fell 13.3 percentage points in New York and 12.5 percentage points in California, while those of natives fell 2.4 points in New York and 3.0 points in California.

Immigrants also experienced greater increases in real median family income during the same period. After adjustment for inflation, the median family income of immigrants rose 26.3 percent from 1994 to 2000, while the median family income of U.S. natives grew half that fast. For recent immigrants, the growth in real median family income was even large: 40.5 percent, an increase of more than $10,000 over the 1994–2000 period. . . .

Share and Income Effects

The share effect is largely driven by the magnitude of the increase in the immigrant share of the population. Nationally, this share grew by 2.6 percentage points between 1994 and 2000. The share of the population consisting of recent immigrants grew less than 1 percentage point during the same period. In New York, the immigrant share of the population grew by 3.6 percentage points, in California by 1.2 percentage points. . . .

The decline in immigrant poverty rates (the income effect), however, more than offset the share effect, so the net result was that immigration *lowered* poverty for each group. Take,

Immigrants Not Driving Nation's Poverty Rate

Immigrants do experience more poverty than native-born citizens, but they are not driving the nation's poverty rate.

In addition, the overall drop in the poverty rate and the rise in national median income in 2006, compared with 2005, were driven by improvement among Hispanics. Hispanic poverty fell, and the median income of Hispanic households rose. Non-Hispanic whites and African Americans, by contrast, experienced no such improvement.

Indeed, since 2001, Hispanics have made considerably more progress against poverty than the other groups. Their poverty rate is lower than it was in 2000, before the last recession—it stands at its lowest level on record—while poverty rates for non-Hispanic whites and blacks remain well above their pre-recession levels.

Robert J. Greenstein, "Misreading the Poverty Data,"
Washington Post, *September 18, 2007, p. A19. Copyright © 2007*
The Washington Post Company. Reproduced by permission.

for example, the case of California. Although the share effect added three-tenths of a percentage point to the poverty rate, the income effect—the fall in immigrant poverty in California—contributed 3.2 percentage points to poverty's decline. The net impact of immigration on California poverty was to lower the State's rate by 2.9 percentage points. For New York, the result was less dramatic, because, whereas the immigrant poverty rate fell steeply, the share grew more quickly than in California and thus added just under a point to the change in poverty between 1994 and 2000. Here, too, however, the poverty-reducing impact of the income effect more than offset the share effect. . . .

Immigration is by no means the whole story in understanding trends over the 1990s. On the basis of a simple shift-share analysis, once the impact of the growth of immigration is extracted, poverty is seen to have been unchanged over the decade in California and to have risen slightly in New York. Given the acknowledged economic prosperity of the 1990s, this finding implies that, as the census data are released and scrutinized, researchers cannot simply cite the increase in immigration as the only or the chief cause of the standstill in poverty rates and leave it at that. Other factors were responsible and need to be understood as well.

Economic Factors to Blame

Although the boom of the latter 1990s lifted low incomes, census data reveal that economic progress by-passed some demographic groups, particularly in certain States. With very little analysis, some commentators have cited increased immigration as the sole or the chief causative factor of flat poverty rates. By contrast, while no analysis could completely account for the effects of immigration (both positive and negative), the one presented in this article indicates that poverty rates would have been only slightly lower, and median income only slightly higher, between 1994 and 2000 if immigration rates had remained constant.

The preliminary analysis of the 1989–99 period yields a similar conclusion. Although data limitations suggest that the results be viewed with caution, it is still the case that, had immigration not increased between 1989 and 1999, poverty rates would not have fallen in California and would have increased slightly in New York.

None of the preceding discussion should be taken to imply that immigration plays *no* role in the economic trends of the 1990s, but, thus far, immigration's role appears to have been overstated at the expense of other, more fundamentally economic factors. Both New York and California, for example, saw larger-than-average increases in inequality over the decade, and the incomes of the wealthy pulled far ahead of those at the middle and the bottom of the income scale. In many States, the increase in inequality meant that the growth that did occur went disproportionately to those at the top of the income scale, leaving those at the lower end more vulnerable to poverty, regardless of their status as natives or immigrants.

The 1990s economic boom arrived later in New York and California than it did in the rest of the United States. For example, unemployment in New York City was 8 percent in 1998, compared with 4.5 percent for the Nation. The fact that unemployment remained high for a time in New York City meant that *all* less advantaged workers, not just immigrants, faced a slack labor market. Any defensible accounting of the trends in income and poverty over the 1990s needs to include at least these explanations and probably others as well.

"We cannot solve the problem of poverty
. . . unless we honestly unravel the complex and continuing connection between poverty and race."

Racism Causes Poverty

Alan Jenkins

*In the following viewpoint, Alan Jenkins claims that while the
open hostility and "whites only" laws of the Jim Crow era have
disappeared, subtle and persistent discrimination against people
of color is a major reason why the poverty rate among African
Americans and Latinos is 2.6 times greater than that among
whites. People of color, he maintains, are far more likely than
whites to be cut off from "quality schools, housing, health care,
consumer credit, and other pathways out of poverty." Jenkins de-
plores the portrayal of poor African Americans in particular as
"dysfunctional and undeserving of assistance," a stereotype that
unfairly blames poor blacks for their plight. Alan Jenkins is the
executive director of The Opportunity Agenda, a communica-
tions and advocacy organization based in New York City that
works to influence public opinion on social justice issues such as*

racial equality, labor rights, and health care. He is also coeditor of All Things Being Equal: Instigating Opportunity in an Inequitable Time.

As you read, consider the following questions:

1. What research does Jenkins present to show that employers' hiring practices discriminate against African Americans?

2. What "invisible" discriminatory practices bar people of color from quality housing near good jobs and schools, according to the author?

3. How do the mainstream media perpetuate unflattering stereotypes of poor black Americans, in Jenkins's view?

Many Americans of goodwill who want to reduce poverty believe that race is no longer relevant to understanding the problem, or to fashioning solutions for it. This view often reflects compassion as well as pragmatism. But we cannot solve the problem of poverty—or, indeed, be the country that we aspire to be—unless we honestly unravel the complex and continuing connection between poverty and race.

Since our country's inception, race-based barriers have hindered the fulfillment of our shared values and many of these barriers persist today. Experience shows, moreover, that reductions in poverty do not reliably reduce racial inequality, nor do they inevitably reach low-income people of color. Rising economic tides do not reliably lift all boats.

In 2000, after a decade of remarkable economic prosperity, the poverty rate among African Americans and Latinos taken together was still 2.6 times greater than that for white Americans. This disparity was stunning, yet it was the smallest difference in poverty rates between whites and others in more than three decades. And from 2001 to 2003, as the economy slowed, poverty rates for most communities of color increased more dramatically than they did for whites, widening the racial poverty gap. From 2004 to 2005, while the overall number of poor Americans declined by almost 1 million, to 37 million, poverty rates for most communities of color actually increased. Reductions in poverty do not inevitably close racial poverty gaps, nor do they reach all ethnic communities equally.

Poor people of color are also increasingly more likely than whites to find themselves living in high-poverty neighborhoods with limited resources and limited options. An analysis by The Opportunity Agenda and the Poverty & Race Research Action Council found that while the percentage of Americans of all races living in high-poverty neighborhoods (those with 30 percent or more residents living in poverty) declined between 1960 and 2000, the racial gap grew considerably. Low-income Latino families were three times as likely as low-income white families to live in these neighborhoods in 1960, but 5.7 times as likely in 2000. Low-income blacks were 3.8 times more likely than poor whites to live in high-poverty neighborhoods in 1960, but 7.3 times more likely in 2000.

These numbers are troubling not because living among poor people is somehow harmful in itself, but because concentrated high-poverty communities are far more likely to be cut off from quality schools, housing, health care, affordable consumer credit, and other pathways out of poverty. And African Americans and Latinos are increasingly more likely than whites to live in those communities. Today, low-income blacks are more than three times as likely as poor whites to be in "deep poverty"—meaning below half the poverty line—while poor Latinos are more than twice as likely.

Persistence of Discrimination

Modern and historical forces combine to keep many communities of color disconnected from networks of economic opportunity and upward mobility. Among those forces is persistent racial discrimination that, while subtler than in past decades, continues to deny opportunity to millions of Americans. Decent employment and housing are milestones on the road out of poverty. Yet these are areas in which racial discrimination stubbornly persists. While the open hostility and "Whites Only" signs of the Jim Crow era have largely disappeared, research shows that identically qualified candidates for jobs and housing enjoy significantly different opportunities depending on their race.

In one study, researchers submitted identical résumés by mail for more than 1,300 job openings in Boston and Chicago, giving each "applicant" either a distinctively "white-sounding" or "black-sounding" name—for instance, "Brendan Baker" versus "Jamal Jones." Résumés with white-sounding names were 50 percent more likely than those with black-sounding names to receive callbacks from employers. Similar research in California found that Asian American and, especially, Arab American résumés received the least-favorable treatment compared to other groups. In recent studies in Milwaukee and New York City, meanwhile, live "tester pairs" with comparable qualifications but of differing races tested not only the effect of race on job prospects but also the impact of an apparent criminal record. In Milwaukee, whites reporting a criminal record were more likely to receive a callback from employers than were blacks without a criminal record. In New York, Latinos and African Americans without criminal records received fewer callbacks than did similarly situated whites, and at rates comparable to whites with a criminal record.

Similar patterns hamper the access of people of color to quality housing near good schools and jobs. Research by the U.S. Department of Housing and Urban Development (HUD) shows that people of color receive less information from real-estate agents, are shown fewer units, and are frequently steered away from predominantly white neighborhoods. In addition to identifying barriers facing African Americans and Latinos, this research found significant levels of discrimination against

Asian Americans, and that Native American renters may face the highest discrimination rates (up to 29 percent) of all.

This kind of discrimination is largely invisible to its victims, who do not know that they have received inaccurate information or been steered away from desirable neighborhoods and jobs. But its influence on the perpetuation of poverty is nonetheless powerful.

Legacy of Past Discrimination

These modern discriminatory practices often combine with historical patterns. In New Orleans, for example, as in many other cities, low-income African Americans were intentionally concentrated in segregated, low-lying neighborhoods and public-housing developments at least into the 1960s. In 2005, when Hurricane Katrina struck and the levees broke, black neighborhoods were most at risk of devastation. And when HUD announced that it would close habitable public-housing developments in New Orleans rather than clean and reopen them, it was African Americans who were primarily prevented from returning home and rebuilding. This and other failures to rebuild and invest have exacerbated poverty—already at high levels—among these New Orleanians.

In the case of Native Americans, a quarter of whom are poor, our government continues to play a more flagrant role in thwarting pathways out of poverty. Unlike other racial and ethnic groups, most Native Americans are members of sovereign tribal nations with a recognized status under our Constitution. High levels of Native American poverty derive not only from a history of wars, forced relocations, and broken treaties by the United States but also from ongoing breaches of trust— like our government's failure to account for tens of billions of dollars that it was obligated to hold in trust for Native American individuals and families. After more than a decade of litigation, and multiple findings of governmental wrongdoing, the United States is trying to settle these cases for a tiny fraction of what it owes.

The Illusion of Racial Equality

Predominant white attitudes at the turn of the millennium are well summarized by the comments of a white respondent to a survey conducted by *Essence* magazine. "No place that I'm aware of," wrote the respondent, "makes [black] people ride on the back of the bus or use a different restroom in this day and age. We got the message; we made the corrections—get on with it."

America has made the necessary racial "corrections" and now its time for blacks "to get on with it?" Tell it to the black job applicants of Boston and Chicago.

In a [2002] field experiment ... researchers Marianne Bertrand of the University of Chicago and Sendhill Mullainathan of the Massachusetts Institute of Technology sent out 5,000 resumes in response to help-wanted ads in Boston and Chicago newspapers. Each resume was randomly assigned either a very black-sounding name (such as "Lakisha Washington" or "Jamal Jones") or a very white-sounding name (such as "Emily Walsh" or "Brendan Baker"). This racial "manipulation," the researchers found, "produced a significant gap in the rate of callbacks for interviews." White names received roughly 50 percent more callbacks than black names. For white applicants, moreover, sending higher quality resumes increased the number of callbacks by 30 percent. For black names, higher-quality resumes elicited no significant callback premium. . . .

Paul Street, Z Magazine,
December 22, 2002.

The trust-fund cases, of course, are just the latest in a string of broken promises by our government. But focusing as they do on dollars and cents, they offer an important window into the economic status that Native American communities and tribes might enjoy today if the U.S. government lived up to its legal and moral obligations.

Meanwhile, the growing diversity spurred by new immigrant communities adds to the complexity of contemporary poverty. Asian American communities, for example, are culturally, linguistically, and geographically diverse, and they span a particularly broad socioeconomic spectrum.

Census figures from 2000 show that while one-third of Asian American families have annual incomes of $75,000 or more, one-fifth have incomes of less than $25,000. While the Asian American poverty rate mirrored that of the country as a whole, Southeast Asian communities reflected far higher levels. Hmong men experienced the highest poverty level (40.3 percent) of any racial group in the nation.

Race and Public Attitudes

Americans' complex attitudes and emotions about race are crucial to understanding the public discourse about poverty and the public's will to address it. Researchers such as Martin Gilens and Herman Gray have repeatedly found that the mainstream media depict poor people as people of color—primarily African Americans—at rates far higher than their actual representation in the population. And that depiction, the research finds, interacts with societal biases to erode support for antipoverty programs that could reach all poor people.

Gilens found, for instance, that while blacks represented only 29 percent of poor Americans at the time he did his research, 65 percent of poor Americans shown on television news were black. In a more detailed analysis of TV newsmagazines in particular, Gilens found a generally unflattering framing of the poor, but the presentation of poor African Americans was more negative still. The most "sympathetic" subgroups of the poor—such as the working poor and the elderly—were underrepresented on these shows, while unemployed working-age adults were overrepresented. And those disparities were greater for African Americans than for others, creating an even more unflattering (and inaccurate) picture of the black poor.

Gray similarly found that poor African Americans were depicted as especially dysfunctional and undeserving of assistance, with an emphasis on violence, poor choices, and dependency. As Gray notes, "The black underclass appears as a menace and a source of social disorganization in news accounts of black urban crime, gang violence, drug use, teenage pregnancy, riots, homelessness, and general aimlessness. In news accounts . . . poor blacks (and Hispanics) signify a social menace that must be contained."

Research also shows that Americans are more likely to blame the plight of poverty on poor people themselves, and less likely to support antipoverty efforts, when they perceive that the people needing help are black. These racial effects are especially pronounced when the poor person in the story is a black single mother. In one study, more than twice the number of respondents supported individual solutions (like the one that says poor people "should get a job") over societal solutions (such as increased education or social services) when the single mother was black.

This research should not be surprising. Ronald Reagan, among others, effectively used the "racialized" mental image of the African American "welfare queen" to undermine support for antipoverty efforts. And the media face of welfare recipients has long been a black one, despite the fact that African Americans have represented a minority of the welfare population. But this research also makes clear that unpacking and disputing racial stereotypes is important to rebuilding a shared sense of responsibility for reducing poverty in all of our communities.

| "*Among those who finish high school, get married, have children only within a marriage and go to work, the odds of long-term poverty are virtually nil.*"

People Are Poor Through Their Own Behavior and Bad Choices

Blake Bailey

Tha National Center for Policy Analysis (NCPA) is a conservative Washington, DC, think tank that opposes government regulations and controls and promotes private-sector, entrepreneurial solutions to social problems such as health care, environmental pollution, poverty, and crime. In the following viewpoint, NCPA intern Blake Bailey uses Census Bureau data to argue that people can pull themselves out of poverty, or minimize their chances of falling into poverty in the first place, simply by graduating from high school, working full-time, and not having children out-of-wedlock. Personal initiative is key, Bailey maintains, and only those government programs that encourage behavioral change— for example, welfare reform that requires a return to work— should be supported.

As you read, consider the following questions:

1. According to Bailey, what is the long-term poverty rate among high school dropouts?

2. What is the poverty rate among never-married households with two or more children, compared with the poverty rate among married households with two or more children, according to the author?

3. Children born to unmarried parents will spend how much of their lives in poverty, as reported by Bailey?

About 31 million Americans live in households with incomes below the poverty level, according to the latest U.S. Census data. Poverty is more than a lack of income. It is also the consequence of specific behaviors and decisions. The 2001 Census data clearly show that dropping out of high school, staying single, having children without a spouse, working only part time or not working at all substantially increase the chances of long-term poverty. Certain behaviors are a recipe for success. Among those who finish high school, get married, have children only within a marriage and go to work, the odds of long-term poverty are virtually nil.

Stay in School

Simply completing high school greatly increases a person's chances of not being poor. The Census Bureau reports that:

- Only 9.6 percent of high school graduates are poor, compared to 22.2 percent of those without a diploma.

- Of those people who complete some college, only 6.6 percent fall below the poverty line.

- This drops to 3.3 percent of those with a bachelor's degree or higher.

Furthermore, these lower propensities for poverty last throughout a person's life. In every adult age group, people who fail to obtain a high school degree are more than twice as likely to fall into poverty. People ages 25 to 54 are nearly three times as likely.

The numbers are worse for long-term poverty—poverty that lasts for years. An Organization for Economic Cooperation and Development (OECD) report found that in the United States:

- High school dropouts suffer a long-term poverty rate of 14.2 percent, while high school grads have only a 3.8 percent long-term poverty rate.

- Only 1.2 percent of adults receiving some education beyond high school are poor long-term.

Get a Job

Despite concerns about the working poor, most people who work full time, even at minimum wage jobs, avoid poverty:

- Only 2.6 percent of people 16 years or older with full time jobs are poor, according to Census data.

- By contrast, 11.4 percent of part-time workers fall under the poverty line, and 20.8 percent of those who do not work fall below the poverty line.

The advantages of work hold true even for at-risk groups, such as single mothers:

- About 83 percent of single mothers who do not work are in poverty, compared to nearly 60 percent who work part time.

- But less than 18 percent of single mothers who work full time are in poverty.

Working also significantly reduces long-term poverty. According to an analysis of the Census Bureau's Survey of Income and Program Participation, 10.8 percent of adults who

The Poor Do Not Work Enough

It's not that the adults who head families in poverty don't earn enough; they don't work enough. Left-wing critics often charge that nowadays "work doesn't work" in our "broken" economic system, by which they mean that wages are so wretched that the poor can't lift themselves up, even when employed. But the [Census Bureau 2006 American Community Survey] informs us that an adult working full-time heads up fewer than 16 percent of all impoverished New York households (and just slightly more than 16 percent nationwide). Among single-woman-headed households, just 14 percent work full-time; 55 percent don't work at all.

True, it may be hard to work full-time as a single mother unless you can afford child care. Yet in New York, ever more women—especially poor women—are choosing to have kids without a husband. The census shows that about 36,000 women annually in New York are now having children out of wedlock. That's one-third of all births in the city, though the data vary widely by race, with Asian-Americans having the lowest out-of-wedlock rate (8 percent) and blacks the highest (62 percent). Most shocking, perhaps, is that more than half of women having children out of wedlock are already in poverty or wind up there within a year of giving birth. . . .

Sociologists will point out (at least in their candid moments) that most people can stay out of poverty in America by doing just a few simple things—most importantly, graduating from high school and not having kids without a spouse on hand. The latest census survey reinforces this basic wisdom.

Steven Malanga, "The Truth About Poverty," www.city-journal.com, Winter 2007. Copyright © The Manhattan Institute. Reproduced by permission.

do not work are poor over the long term. In contrast, only 1.7 percent of those employed part time stay poor for extended periods. People employed full time have a 0.4 percent chance of long-term poverty.

Moreover, the government can encourage behavioral changes. Research shows that between one-third and one-half of the fall in poverty among single mothers on welfare after 1994 was due to the 1996 welfare reforms that encouraged work.

Get Married

Marriage is also a strong deterrent to poverty.

- Only 4.0 percent of married couples without children are in poverty, according to Census data.

- In contrast, the poverty rate for singles without children is 8.6 percent.

Moreover, married couples are less likely to experience long-term poverty. According to the OECD report:

- Married couples without children have a long-term poverty rate of only 1.3 percent.

- By contrast, 7.9 percent of single adults experience long-term poverty.

Marriage promotes economic advancement. One study found that married men earn 22 percent more than their unmarried counterparts. The OECD reports that a woman head of household who marries increases her chances of exiting poverty by 23 percent. A single person who marries and finds employment increases his or her chances of leaving poverty by over 50 percentage points.

No Children Out of Wedlock

Having children outside of marriage is costly for both the individual and the child. The Census Bureau reports:

- Of those households with two or more children under the age of 18, 7.9 percent of married households were poor, while 51.6 percent of never-married households were poor.

- Of those households with two or more children under the age of 6, 11.5 percent of married households were poor, while 62.4 percent of never-married households were poor.

According to the OECD study, spells of poverty are 12.6 percent shorter for married households compared to female-headed households. Similarly, married households with children are much more likely to avoid long-term poverty than single parent households. Only 1.7 percent of married households with children suffer long-term poverty, while 26 percent of single parent households are poor long term.

Child poverty is dependent on the behavior of parents. Using data from the National Longitudinal Survey of Youth, a Heritage Foundation study finds:

- On average, a child raised by a never-married mother is 9 times more likely to live in poverty than a child raised by two parents in an intact marriage.

- Nearly 80 percent of children in long-term poverty live in some type of broken family or with a never-married parent.

- Children born to parents who do not marry spend, on average, 56.7 percent of their lives in poverty as opposed to just 6.3 percent for children in married families.

Encourage Poverty-Reducing Behavior

Poverty is most often a consequence of specific behavior. By engaging in other behaviors, people can avoid poverty. To help people escape poverty, government programs should encourage these behaviors. The 1996 welfare reforms encouraged work—and the rate of poverty fell. Proposals to encourage marriage . . . could have similar benefits.

"Now that there are no jobs to go around, there is no safety net for millions of the most vulnerable members of American society."

Massive Job Loss Is Increasing Poverty in America

John Peterson

John Peterson is the editor of the Socialist Appeal, *the journal of the Socialist Workers International League, formed in 2003 to further labor unions and immigrant rights and oppose capitalist exploitation of American workers. In the following viewpoint, Peterson blames job loss (primarily manufacturing jobs) for rising poverty rates so severe that 31 million Americans are not sure they will have enough to eat in the year ahead. According to Peterson, the severity of the labor slump is obscured by the federal government, which excludes from unemployment figures those people who have given up actively looking for work—in fact, he says, the slump is the longest, and has affected the most people, since job numbers were first compiled in 1939.*

As you read, consider the following questions:

1. According to Peterson, what accounts for the difference between the actual U.S. unemployment rate and the reported rate of 6.0 percent?

2. How long, on average, does a person remain unemployed following job loss, according to the author?

3. How has the problem of unemployment and poverty been exacerbated by both Republican and Democratic administrations, in Peterson's view?

The crisis of unemployment and poverty in America continues to worsen. Despite a nominal increase in jobs in [early 2006], what is not reported is what kind of jobs are being created. Manufacturing jobs, the backbone of any economy, continued to be lost. . . . For the vast majority of Americans, the days of high-quality jobs with decent wages, security, and full health and retirement benefits are a thing of the past. The effect this is having in terms of unemployment, homelessness, and even hunger right here in the U.S. is a devastating indictment of a system which places profits before human need and suffering.

True Extent of Unemployment

So although the unemployment figure dropped from 6.1 percent to 6.0 percent, the real situation is being concealed by the government's "revised" method of compiling the figures. According to a report on "Understanding the Severity of the Current Labor Slump" by Lee Price with Yulia Fungard, a number of factors must be considered in order to understand the severity of the current labor slump:

> The record length of time that jobs have failed to recover. Prior to the current slump, jobs had never fallen over a two-and-a-half-year period since monthly job numbers began in 1939. As of October 2003, payroll jobs had fallen by 2.4 million below the level of March 2001.

The growth in the working age population since the recession began in March 2001. Even as jobs were shrinking by 1.8 percent, the working-age population (i.e., the number of people of working age) was growing by 3.4 percent. Had job growth kept up with working age population growth over that period, 6.9 million more payroll jobs would have been filled in October 2003.

The effect of the "missing" labor market on the unemployment rate. The unusually prolonged loss of jobs has caused an unprecedented number of people to refrain from actively looking for work, and therefore to be excluded from the unemployment measurement. Had the labor force grown more in line with the population—as it has in past labor slumps—another 2.3 million people would have been in the labor force in October 2003.

This "missing" labor force is significant because the unemployment rate would have been 7.4 percent had the 2.3 million "missing" workers been considered as unemployed. The 7.4 percent unemployment figure provides a better measure of current slack in the labor market than the actual unemployment rate of 6.0 percent. The 1.4 percentage-point difference reflects the people pushed to the sidelines of the labor market who can be expected to seek work again once job prospects improve. As a result, the official unemployment rate should not be expected to fall very much when the employment picture actually begins to improve.

The loss of wage and salary income. Although real hourly wages have grown since the start of the recession, those gains have been more than offset by declines in the number of jobs and the amount of hours paid per job.

This slump saw the longest duration of job loss—28 months.

This slump is the first time in which there was not a full recovery of Jobs 31 months after the recession began.

This slump is the worst in terms of the rise of the unemployment rate (after adjustment for the "missing" labor force) 31 months after the recession began—up 3.2 percentage points.

The current slump has also been the most severe in terms of the loss of aggregate real wage and salary income 30 months after the recession began—down 1.2 percent.

Job Loss Raises Poverty Rate

According to the authors of this study, because of the extended period of job loss, the current labor slump is the most severe on record by several important measures. And this is the very best this system has to offer!

In the year 2002, 1.7 million Americans slipped below the poverty line, bringing the total to 34.6 million. That's an astonishing one in eight of the population. Over 13 million of them are children. In fact, the U.S. has the worst child poverty rate and the worst life expectancy of all the world's industrialized countries, and the plight of its poor is worsening. Thirty one million Americans were deemed to be "food insecure" (they literally did not know where their next meal was coming from). Of those, more than nine million were categorized by the U.S. Department of Agriculture as experiencing real hunger, defined by the U.S. Department of Agriculture as an "uneasy or painful sensation caused by lack of food due to lack of resources to obtain food."

In 25 major cities the need for emergency food rose an average of 19 percent [in 2005]. The number of Americans on food stamps has risen from 17 million to 22 million since [President George W.] Bush took office. There are more Americans living in poverty now than there were in 1965. What happened to "progress" and things getting better from generation to generation? What is Bush's solution? "Faith-based" charities!

The Downside of the "Churning" Economy

Robert Kimmitt of the U.S. Treasury points out that 55 million Americans left their jobs in 2006. Kimmitt also notes 57 million people were hired during the same period. Praising this so called "churning" of the labor market Kimmitt suggests this is a sign of a healthy economy because it reflects the movement of people in response to opportunity. . . .

Kimmitt speaks of the upside, but is there also a downside to this process of churning? According the Bureau of Labor Statistics data on layoffs and plant closures, in rural areas particularly, churning is liable to result in long periods of unemployment, forced shifts to other industries and lower wages once the tumultuous journey is over.

Amy K. Glasmeier,
Poverty in America, January 26, 2007.
www.povertyinamerica.psu.edu.

Valuing Profit over People

And the Democrats are no better. Let's not forget that it was [President Bill] Clinton who dismantled the system of social welfare we fought for in the 1930s and '60s. He slashed the welfare rolls from 12 to 5 million in a matter of years, and now that there are no jobs to go around, there is no safety net for millions of the most vulnerable members of American society. But the fact of the matter is, we don't want welfare. We want quality jobs, health care, housing, and education, and we don't mind working hard to get these things. But the capitalist system is based on the endless pursuit of profit—our interests come second to the interests of the CEOs and billionaires.

And this in the richest country in the world! So where is all the wealth workers create going? It's no mystery—it's all in the hands of a tiny minority of ultra-wealthy parasites who leech off our hard work, blood, sweat, and tears. There is absolutely no material reason why we can't have full employment, free universal health care and education, and much, much more. But to get this we need to fight for it—the capitalist class and their political representatives are not going to give up their wealth, power, and privileges without a fight. This is why we need to work towards building a mass party of labor which can genuinely fight in our interests. By basing itself on the unions and the working class generally (the vast majority of American society), such a party could rapidly come to political power and fight to implement a socialist program to improve the lives of everyone. The fact that voter turnout is generally so low shows just how frustrated Americans are with the choices being offered. Nowhere does it say that we must choose between the two parties of the rich. This is not real democracy!

Periodical Bibliography

The following articles have been selected to supplement the diverse views presented in this chapter.

Steven A. Camarota and Gerald D. Jaynes — "Domestic Poverty: Should Immigration Be Reduced to Protect the Jobs of Native-Born Poor?" *CQ Researcher*, September 7, 2007.

Erik Eckholm — "Blue-Collar Jobs Disappear, Taking Families' Way of Life Along," *New York Times*, January 16, 2008.

Edward L. Glaeser, Matthew E. Kahn, and Jordan Rappaport — "Why Do the Poor Live in Cities?" *Journal of Urban Economics*, January 2008.

Terry D. Goddard — "Culture War or Blame Game? Debating Race and Poverty," *Journal of Urban History*, November 2006.

Brian Grow and Keith Epstein — "The Poverty Business: Inside U.S. Companies' Audacious Drive to Extract More Profits from the Nation's Working Poor," *Business Week*, May 21, 2007.

Hilary W. Hoynes, Marianne E. Page, and Ann Huff Stevens — "Poverty in America: Trends and Explanations," *Journal of Economic Perspectives*, Winter 2006.

Robert M. Kimmitt — "Why Job Chum Is Good," *Washington Post*, January 23, 2007.

Michael Miller — "Population and Poverty," *Acton Commentary*, Acton Institute, May 30, 2007. www.acton.org/commentary/commentary385.php.

Mark R. Rank — "Toward a New Understanding of American Poverty," *Journal of Law & Policy*, Washington University in St. Louis, vol. 20, no. 17, 2006.

William E. Spriggs — "The Changing Face of Poverty in America: Why Are So Many Women, Children, Racial and Cultural Minorities Still Poor?" *American Prospect*, May 2007.

CHAPTER 3

How Can Poverty Be Reduced in the United States?

Chapter Preface

In September 2007, New York City mayor Michael Bloomberg launched a pilot antipoverty program that has never before been tried in the United States. Opportunity NYC is a type of antipoverty initiative known as Conditional Cash Transfers (CCTs). In a speech at the Brookings Center on Children and Families, Bloomberg explained how it works:

> We'll begin making cash payments—from privately raised dollars—to a test group of young people and adults *if*—let me say that again—*if* they do the things that are most likely to lead them to break the cycle of poverty. That means high school students will be able to earn $600 for each statewide standardized test they pass, $400 for graduating, and up to $50 a month for maintaining near-perfect school attendance, while adults will be able to earn up to $150 a month for working full-time.

CCTs, established since the 1990s first in Mexico and now in about twenty countries, have produced documented reductions in the incidence of poverty and malnutrition and improvements in school enrollment and completion. But the launch of Opportunity NYC has provoked vigorous opposition on moral and practical grounds. Some critics charge that CCTs take capitalism's reward-for-work ethic too far and undermine the development of individual responsibility. Others predict that irresponsible parents will have more children to get more money, or use payments to benefit themselves instead of their children. And others draw the line at the prospect of eventually using taxpayer dollars to fund the program. But Bloomberg strongly defended the controversial plan:

> You might say "But why should we pay people for doing what they're supposed to do?" . . . Think of it this way: Every other antipoverty program that's been tried has failed to

get the national poverty rate below 11 percent. So what are the options? Do nothing? Or dress up the failed old ideas? We have other options, but only if we're not afraid of thinking outside the box, even if that means breaking taboos.

The viewpoints in this chapter debate traditional and innovative antipoverty strategies in the effort to do what Opportunity NYC aims to do.

> "Raising the minimum wage ... would
> ensure ... that a family of four with a
> parent working full-time at the mini-
> mum wage does not have to raise its
> children in poverty."

Raising the Minimum Wage Will Reduce Poverty

Jason Furman and Sharon Parrot

Jason Furman is a senior fellow at the Brookings Institution, a nonpartisan Washington, DC, think tank where he directs the Hamilton Project, an initiative that promotes economic growth. Sharon Parrot is the director of the Welfare Reform and Income Support Division of the Center of Budget and Policy Priorities in Washington. In the following viewpoint, Furman and Parrot argue that although the government poverty line is a useful measure of income inadequacy, meeting basic needs is a struggle for millions of people at and above this income calculation. Today's housing, child-care, and health-care costs are far higher than poverty calculations take into account, they maintain, and a higher minimum wage is an essential step in keeping more people from sliding into poverty as well as being an important complement to government benefits issued to the working poor.

Jason Furman and Sharon Parrot, "A $7.25 Minimum Wage Would Be a Useful Step in Helping Working Families Escape Poverty," www.cbpp.org, January 5, 2007. Reproduced by permission.

As you read, consider the following questions:

1. What do Furman and Parrot consider a reasonable minimum hourly wage?
2. Why would some larger families remain below the poverty line even if the minimum wage is raised to the authors' recommended level?
3. What percentage of income does the government estimate Americans spend on housing, and what percentage do they actually spend on housing, according to Furman and Parrot?

In the early 1990s there was basic agreement that parents working full time should not have to raise their children in poverty. While liberals and conservatives sometimes differed on the means to reach this goal, they agreed with the core principle.

The yardstick used to measure achievement of this goal was whether a minimum-wage earner in a family of four earned enough (after subtraction of payroll taxes), together with the Earned Income Tax Credit (EITC) and food stamps, to have an income at or above the poverty line. (It should be noted that this is a very low floor. In 2006, the federal poverty line for a family of four was about $20,000, well short of what most Americans would consider a decent standard of living.)...

This goal was reached in the late 1990s, as a result of an EITC increase enacted in 1993 and a minimum-wage increase enacted in 1996. In 1998, a typical family of four with a full-time, minimum-wage worker had income above the poverty line when food stamps and EITC benefits were considered.

However, ten years of inflation have eroded the minimum wage to its lowest inflation-adjusted level in more than 50 years. As a result, in 2006 a family of four with one minimum-wage earner had a total income (including food stamps and the EITC) of $18,950, some $1,550 *below* the poverty line.

Raising the minimum wage from its current level of $5.15 an hour [$5.85 as of July 24, 2007] to $7.25 in 2009, as has been proposed, would ensure once more that a family of four with a parent working full time at the minimum wage does not have to raise its children in poverty. The increase would mean an additional $4,200 in annual earnings for a full-time, minimum-wage worker. It also would automatically trigger $1,140 in increases in the family's EITC and refundable Child Tax Credit, enough to roughly offset the decrease in the family's food stamp benefits resulting from the increase in the family's cash income. As a result, the family would be lifted 5 percent *above* the poverty line, instead of being 11 percent *below* the poverty line in 2009, as it would be under current [pre–July 2007] law.

It is important to note that if, as is expected, the minimum wage legislation does not index the wage for inflation after 2009, inflation will once again begin to erode the wage's value. If no other changes are made, the family in this example will fall back below the poverty line by 2015.

Some Minimum-Wage Workers Will Remain Poor

While an increase in the minimum wage would raise the earnings of many workers and lift some families above the poverty line, some minimum-wage workers would remain poor. This includes many workers who experience periods of joblessness during the year. Low-wage workers often are ineligible for unemployment insurance when they lose their jobs; even when they are eligible, they often receive low benefits.

Moreover, some larger families with a full-time, minimum-wage worker would not be lifted above the poverty line by an increase in the minimum wage, even if they receive food stamps and the refundable tax credits for which they are eligible. While families with more children have larger needs—which is why the poverty line is set higher for larger families—wages (including the minimum wage) do *not* rise with family size. As a result, the poverty rate for families with three or more children is more than double the rate for families with one or two children.

Even with a $7.25-an-hour minimum wage, a family of five with a full-time, minimum-wage earner that receives food stamps and the refundable tax credits would fall $1,139 below the poverty line in 2009. Families of more than five would fall even farther below the poverty line. In part, this reflects the fact that while a larger EITC is provided to families with *two* or more children than to families with one child, no additional adjustment is provided for families with three or more children. (Various policy analysts have called for such adjustment, and policymakers as diverse as former Rep. Dick Armey and President Bill Clinton have proposed it, but it has not been enacted.). . .

While the goal of lifting working families to the poverty line is a worthy one, families with incomes *just above* the poverty line also face real difficulties making ends meet. The poverty line was established in the 1960s and was calculated by multiplying the cost of feeding a family by three, under the assumption that families spend, on average, one-third of their income on food. The poverty line is a useful measure of income adequacy, particularly because it provides a historical look at the extent to which American's incomes fell above or below a particular standard. But, the standard does not necessarily reflect the cost of raising a family today and families with incomes at the poverty line often struggle to meet their basic needs.

- *Housing.* Housing cost burdens for poor families are often severe, and the cost of housing is likely to take far more than 30 percent of most low-income working families' incomes—the government's standard for housing affordability—even after the minimum-wage increase takes effect. Nationwide, the average cost of a

Minimum Wage Is Far from a Living Wage

In recent years, many economists have pointed out that the poverty rate is calculated with an overly simplistic formula that hasn't changed since the 1960s, and does not include the effect of factors like taxes, home ownership, health care and child care costs.

"There's almost no place in America where you can live on $20,000 as a family of four...you need at least $36,000 to pay basic expenses," said Amy Glasmeier, director of the Poverty in America project at Penn State University, which developed a city-specific Living Wage Calculator based on census data and economic statistics....

Minimum wage is higher in New York than in many other states—it [rose] to $7.15 an hour on Jan. 1, [2007] while the federal rate remains stuck at $5.85—but it's still a far cry from what many people consider a living wage....

"Lower middle income workers, which is what I would call anyone making under $50,000 a year, are feeling really significant constraints based on changing national economic circumstances," Glasmeier said. "They're the first to feel the effect of things like rising gas prices and higher interest rates."

Amanda Bensen, Glens Falls (NY) Post-Star, *August 5, 2006.*

modest two-bedroom apartment in 2006 was $821 per month, or $9,852 per year, according to the U.S. Department of Housing and Urban Development (HUD). At this cost, rent and utilities consume nearly half (48 percent) of the income of a family of four at the poverty line. Even if the proposed minimum-wage increase takes full effect in 2009, the cost of a modest two-bedroom apartment will consume an average of 46 percent of the total income of a family of four with a full-time, minimum-wage worker. (This calculation assumes that the family receives food stamps, the EITC and child tax credit.)

- *Child care.* Many working families face significant child care costs, and quality child care programs can be out of reach for low-income working families. According to the National Association of Child Care Resource and Referral Agencies, in the median state in the 2004–2005 academic year, full-time infant care in a licensed child care center cost an average of $7,100 per year, while full-time care for preschoolers in a licensed child care center cost an average of $5,800. Without a child care subsidy, a family earning at or near the minimum wage is unlikely to be able to afford such a tuition bill for one child, let alone two or more children.

Unfortunately, due to a lack of funding, child care subsidy programs serve only a minority of those eligible for such assistance. Working families that need child care but cannot afford it and do not receive subsidies have few options—they can try to rely on friends and family for care or find lower-cost paid providers that likely offer lower-quality care.

- *Health care.* Most children in families with a full-time, minimum-wage worker are eligible for free or low-cost health insurance through Medicaid or the State Children's Health Insurance Program. However, most low-income working *parents* are not eligible for health insurance through these programs, and few have private coverage. In fact, in 25 states, a parent in a three-person family with a full-time, minimum-wage job earns too much to qualify for Medicaid. Because of the lack of either public or private coverage, about 41 percent of all parents with incomes below the poverty line were uninsured in 2005, according to Census data. Adult low-wage workers who are not parents almost never are eligible for Medicaid coverage unless they have a severe disability. Some 45 percent of poor childless adults are uninsured.

Evidence of the difficulties near-poor households have in making ends meet is found in the U.S. Department of Agriculture's [USDA] "food insecurity" data. In 2005, according to USDA, about one in seven households with incomes between 100 percent and 185 percent of the poverty line were uncertain of having, or unable to acquire, enough food because they had insufficient money and other resources for food.

Building on a Higher Minimum Wage

Raising the minimum wage would be an important first step and a useful complement to public policies like the EITC, food stamps, and child care subsidies, which provide additional benefits and supports for low-income working families. A broader agenda is needed, however, to raise the prospects of low-wage workers and their families more significantly. Such an agenda would need to include additional income supports, help in obtaining the health care, child care, and housing that these families need but often cannot afford, and new opportunities to attend college or upgrade their skills so they can secure higher paying, more stable jobs.

"A 10 percent increase in the minimum wage reduces employment of young workers by 1 percent to 2 percent."

Raising the Minimum Wage Will Not Reduce Poverty

David R. Henderson

In the following viewpoint, researcher David Henderson calculates the negative effects of raising the minimum wage: higher unemployment because employers forced to pay higher wages will discharge the least productive employees and be less likely to hire new workers, a higher high-school dropout rate because teens will see higher wages as enticement to leave school, a rise in poverty because there will be fewer jobs, cuts in employee benefits, and a loss of competition in the marketplace. David Henderson is a fellow at the domestic policy think tank the Hoover Institution, a professor of economics at the Naval Postgraduate School, and the author of Making Great Decisions in Business and Life.

As you read, consider the following questions:

1. According to Henderson, why do minimum-wage laws primarily hurt teenagers and young adults?

2. How many jobs does Henderson estimate would be destroyed by a 15 percent increase in the minimum wage?

3. What ulterior motives does the author attribute to labor unions, which lobby for higher minimum wages along with other worker benefits?

Various state legislators and interest groups around the United States are pushing for increases in the minimum wage. In California, for example, even Republican Gov. Arnold Schwarzenegger [advocated] raising the state minimum wage from its current $6.75 an hour to $7.75 by July 2007. But when the minimum wage law confronts the law of demand, the law of demand wins every time. And the real losers are the most marginal workers—the ones who will be out of a job.

Creates Unemployment

In a free labor market, wage rates reflect the willingness of workers to work (supply) and the willingness of employers to hire them (demand). Worker productivity is the main determinant of what employers are willing to pay. Most working people are not directly affected by the minimum wage because their productivity and, hence, their pay, is already well above it.

The law of demand says that at a higher price, less is demanded, and it applies to grapefruit, cars, movie tickets and, yes, labor. Because a legislated increase in the price of labor does not increase workers' productivity, some workers will lose their jobs. Which ones? Those who are the least productive.

Minimum wage laws mostly harm teenagers and young adults because they typically have little work experience and take jobs that require fewer skills. That's why economists looking for the effect of the minimum wage on employment don't look at data on educated 45-year-old men; rather, they focus on teenagers and young adults, especially black teenagers. Paul

Samuelson, the first American winner of the Nobel Prize in economics, put it succinctly back in 1970. Analyzing a proposal to raise the minimum wage to $2 an hour in his famous textbook, *Economics*, he wrote, "What good does it do a black youth to know that an employer must pay him $2 an hour if the fact that he must be paid that amount is what keeps him from getting a job?"

A comprehensive survey of minimum wage studies found that a 10 percent increase in the minimum wage reduces employment of young workers by 1 percent to 2 percent.

To put that into perspective:

- Gov. Schwarzenegger's proposed 15 percent increase in the state minimum wage would destroy about 35,000 to 70,000 unskilled jobs—putting 1.5 to 3 percent of young Californians out of work.

- Overall, the proposed minimum wage increase in California would eliminate about 70,000 to 140,000 jobs.

- A 15 percent increase in the minimum wage nationwide would destroy about 290,000 to 590,000 young people's jobs, and about 400,000 to 800,000 jobs overall.

Fortunately, and to his credit, Gov. Schwarzenegger wants to avoid indexing the minimum wage to either the consumer price index or a wage index, as the French government did in 1970. Indexing the minimum wage makes it much harder to get the inflation-adjusted minimum wage down and makes it permanently harder for the least-skilled workers to find jobs. The rising minimum wage in France since then has added to the country's youth-unemployment woes.

Encourages Teenagers to Drop Out

Some minimum wage advocates argue that teenagers should be in high school or college anyway—not working—and therefore the loss of jobs for young workers is somehow not very harmful. Ironically, though, economic studies have shown that a higher minimum wage entices some teenage students to drop out. With fewer jobs to go around and a greater number of dropouts, some newer dropouts take jobs from the less-educated and lower-productivity teens who had already left school.

Even worse, the failure to find work early in their lives harms young people later in their work lives. For example, economists David Neumark of the Public Policy Institute of California and Olena Nizalova of Michigan State University found that even people in their late 20s worked less and earned less the longer they were exposed to a high minimum wage, presumably because the minimum wage destroyed job opportunities early in their work life.

Hurts the Poor

Proponents of a higher minimum wage often argue that that it's difficult to support a family when the only breadwinner earns the current minimum wage. This claim is flawed, for three reasons.

First, for a minimum-wage increase to help a single breadwinner earn money for his or her family, the worker must have a job and keep it at this higher wage. A job at $5.15 an hour, the current federal minimum, is much better than no job at $6.00 an hour.

Second, increases in the minimum wage actually redistribute income among poor families by giving some higher wages and putting others out of work. A 1997 National Bureau of Economic Research study estimated that the federal minimum-wage hike of 1996 and 1997 actually increased the number of poor families by 4.5 percent.

Third, a relatively small percentage of the workers directly affected are the sole breadwinner in a family with children. A study by the Employment Policies Institute shows that in California, for example, only 20 percent of the workers who would

Raising the Minimum Wage Destroys Jobs

The usual arguments on behalf of the minimum wage are simply wrong. Rarely do workers support families on the minimum wage. Columnist Mona Charen points to Labor Department data that more than four in five minimum wage recipients have no dependents. Most are second or third earners in a family, not heads of households. Just 1.2 percent hold full-time jobs. Most are below age 25 and almost half of their families earn above $60,000 a year.

Instead of helping those most in need, the minimum wage prevents the most disadvantaged from getting a foot on the ladder of economic success. If you raise the cost of hiring workers, fewer will be hired. If you raise the salary that must be paid, employers will reject those with the least skills, education, and training.

If there is one issue about which economists agree, it is that the minimum wage destroys jobs. Indeed, whatever legislators might say in public, they obviously understand this point. After all, if you could raise wages without consequence, then Congress should up it to $100 or $1,000 an hour and make all of us rich.

The only question about an increase, whether to $7.25 or $1,000, is how many jobs are destroyed. Raising the minimum wage has discouraged employment of minority teens, spurred mechanization, and encouraged substitution of fewer, better-trained workers for unskilled laborers. (This, of course, is why organized labor backs government wage-setting.) In short, the minimum wage, however well intentioned, hurts those it is supposed to help.

Doug Bandow, American Spectator,
January 30, 2007.

have been directly affected by a proposed 2004 minimum-wage increase were supporting a family on a single, minimum-wage income. The other 80 percent were teenagers or adult children living with their parents, adults living alone, or dual earners in a married couple.

Reduces Other Job Benefits

Even when minimum-wage increases don't put low-wage workers out of work, they don't necessarily help them either. The reason: Employers respond to forced higher wages by adjusting other components of employee compensation, such as health insurance or other benefits. Although few minimum wage workers have employer-provided health insurance, employers have found other ways to adjust, such as cutting on-the-job training. In their study of changes in the minimum wage laws between 1981 and 1991, Neumark and Federal Reserve Board member and economist William Wascher concluded, "[M]inimum wages reduce training aimed at improving skills on the current job, especially formal training."

Reduces Competition

The main proponents of the minimum wage are labor union officials who use substantial resources to lobby and testify for higher minimum wages. But they have a self-interested motive: hobbling the competition. Almost all union members make well above the minimum wage, but by getting the minimum wage increased, they can reduce competition from less-skilled workers who would receive lower wages. Similarly, large employers who pay more than the minimum, Wal-Mart being the most recent example, also push for higher minimum wages, presumably to make things more difficult for their low-wage competitors.

In addition to labor unions and major corporations, some politicians also like to advocate a higher minimum wage. Politicians in the Northeast, for example, have traditionally favored high federal minimum wages to stem the flow of jobs from the North to the lower-wage South. Indeed, in 1957, Massachusetts Sen. John Kennedy argued for a higher minimum on the grounds that it would make low-wage black workers in the South less competitive with the higher-wage white workers whom he represented.

Imposes an Employer Mandate

Although economists generally focus on the negative effects of the minimum wage on vulnerable workers, there is another group that also deserves to be considered: employers. How can we justify forcing employers, the very people who are taking risks to provide jobs in the first place, to pay a higher wage? If "society" decides that unskilled people should be paid more, why single out employers rather than, say, taxpayers in general, as the people to pay them?

> "Our country has made great strides
> against poverty . . . [and] with the right
> mix of policies and societal action, we
> can make even greater strides."

Expanding Government Programs Can Reduce Poverty

John Podesta

John Podesta is the president of the Center for American Progress, a progressive political policy and research organization in Washington, DC; a visiting professor of law at Georgetown University Law Center; and former chief of staff to President Bill Clinton from 1998 to 2001. In the following April 2007 congressional testimony, Podesta represents the center in advocating a twelve-step package of government programs that he predicts will cut the U.S. poverty rate in half by 2017. Components of the package include expanding federal tax credits and guaranteeing child care for low-income workers, legislation that promotes workplace unionization, higher education grants, and mortgage assistance. Podesta proposes to pay for these expanded government benefits by levying higher taxes on the wealthiest Americans, who he claims have benefited unfairly from excessive tax cuts in recent years.

John Podesta, "Testimony Before the Subcommittee on Income Security and Family Support of the House Committee on Ways and Means," *U.S. House of Representatives*, April 26, 2007 was created by the Center for American Progress (www.american progress.org). Reproduced by permission.

As you read, consider the following questions:

1. How does Podesta address the charge that expanding federal benefits will make the poor more dependent on welfare handouts?
2. What changes to the Earned Income Tax Credit and Child Tax Credit does the author recommend?
3. How much does Podesta estimate his poverty-reduction plan will cost?

In February of 2006, the Center for American Progress convened a diverse group of national experts and leaders to examine issues of poverty and to make recommendations for national action. . . .

In its report, the Task Force calls for a national goal of cutting poverty in half in the next ten years and proposes a strategy to reach the goal. The report calls for the Congress, the president, and the next administration to join this effort and set our country on a course to end American poverty in a generation. We recommend a strategy that promotes decent work; provides opportunity for all, ensures economic security, and helps people build wealth. . . .

Three Misleading Ideas About Poverty

First, poverty is not just a "poor person's" issue. It affects us all in distinct and important ways. Too often, discussions of poverty are treated as if they're unrelated to the issues facing the middle class. But large numbers of Americans—both low-income and middle class—are increasingly concerned about uncertain job futures, downward pressures on wages, and decreasing opportunities for advancement in a global economy. Employment for millions of Americans is now less secure than at any point in the post–World War II era. Jobs are increasingly unlikely to provide health care coverage and guaranteed pensions. The typical U.S. worker will change jobs numerous times over his or her working years and must adapt to rapid technological change. One-quarter of all jobs in the U.S. economy do not pay enough to support a family of four above the poverty line.

It is in our nation's interest that those jobs be filled and that employment rates be high. It is not in our nation's interest that people working in these jobs be confined to poverty. Large numbers would benefit if more jobs paid enough to support a family. Some issues are distinct, particularly for the smaller group of Americans in long-term, persistent poverty. But much of the agenda to reduce poverty is also one to promote opportunity and security for millions of other Americans, too. Second, poverty is not unconquerable. Our country has made great strides against poverty in the past. With the right mix of policies and societal action, we can make even greater strides in the future. Fueled by years of inaccurate characterizations of past efforts ("We fought a war on poverty and poverty won," as [former president] Ronald Reagan stated) many Americans are left to conclude that little can be done beyond providing private charity and urging the poor to do better. Nothing could be farther from the truth. The United States has seen periods of dramatic poverty reduction. Amid the strong economy of the 1960s and the War on Poverty, the poverty rate fell from 22.4 percent to 11.1 percent between 1959 and 1973. In the 1990s, a strong economy was combined with policies to promote and support work; the poverty rate dropped from 15.1 percent to 11.3 percent between 1993 and 2000. In each period, a near-full employment economy, sound federal and state policies that focused on rewarding work, individual initiative, supportive civic institutions and communities, and a sustained national commitment led to significant progress. In the last six years, our nation has moved in the opposite direction. The number of poor Americans has grown by five million. The federal minimum wage has remained flat. Funding for key federal programs that help people get and keep jobs has been stagnant or worse. Third, fighting poverty does not mean the poor will become more dependent on government. To the contrary, as our Task Force report shows, smart policies to fight poverty will actually increase the value of work and the commitment to work and help low-income families become more economically self-sufficient in the long run. A false argument exists that anything done by the federal government to combat poverty naturally leads to negative consequences. In fact, we know that policies such as the Earned Income Tax Credit and expanded child care provisions encourage work and strong families.

Four Strategic Goals

Therefore, our Task Force has recommended a four-part strategy to fight poverty:

Promote Decent Work. We start from the belief that people should work, and that work should pay enough to ensure that workers and their families can avoid poverty, meet basic needs, and save for the future.

Ensure Opportunity for All. Children should grow up in conditions that maximize their opportunities for success; adults should have opportunities throughout their lives to connect to work, get more education, live in a good neighborhood, and move up in the workforce.

Ensure Economic Security. Americans should not fall into poverty during times when they cannot work or work is unavailable, unstable, or pays too little to make ends meet.

Help People Build Wealth. All Americans should have assets that allow them to weather periods of flux and volatility and to have the resources that may be essential to upward economic mobility.

Our strategy is based on the reality that poverty is complex and that the faces of the poor are many. No single approach or policy solution could viably move huge numbers out of poverty. Good jobs and benefits matter. Solid education matters. Safe and enriching neighborhoods matter. Opportunities to increase assets and wealth matter. Economic security and access to health care matter. Protections for the most vulnerable matter. Personal initiative, strong families, and corporate responsibility matter. We understand that some policymakers highlight the importance of promoting marriage as a strategy for reducing poverty. Research consistently finds that all else being equal, children growing up with both parents in a healthy marriage are more likely to fare better over time in terms of social and educational outcomes. At the same time, all else is often not equal. Children with loving parents can and do thrive in a range of family structures. Government policies should find ways to support marriage, such as eliminating the marriage penalty in the EITC, but they should also support families in ways that recognize the range of settings in which children grow up. In more general terms, our basic strategy is to offer solutions to help replace America's cycle of poverty—the tens of millions of people consigned to destitution every year because of our collective inability and unwillingness to prevent it—with a new cycle of prosperity.

We believe that decent work should be at the center of this new approach. Nothing is more important to the cycle of prosperity than good jobs—with adequate income and benefits—that allow people to take care of their families and start building assets.

Along with a job that pays a livable wage, strong personal character and individual initiative help to build strong and stable families. Strong families, in turn, help to build stable, safe, and caring communities. Communities foster good schools and encourage a culture that takes pride in personal achievement and educational success—all essential elements of economic mobility. Research clearly shows that educational attainment and personal qualities that value success and achievement early in life are directly correlated to higher wages and a better quality of life later in life.

Educational achievement leads to enhanced job prospects and increased earning potential. As wages rise, opportunities to build wealth and assets through increased savings, home-ownership, and small business investments increase one's life prospects and bring additional funds to neighborhoods, communities, and local schools.

As economists and academics have shown, assets provide insurance and cushions against unforeseen economic shocks. They encourage people to focus long term and improve their own intellectual and creative development. They increase self-sufficiency and help people move away from public support. And they encourage people to become active in the actions of government and society. Rising wages and wealth in turn provide new opportunities for the overall economy and a better quality of life in our neighborhoods and communities.

Twelve Steps to Cut Poverty in Half

To flesh out this strategy, we specifically recommend 12 steps for federal, state, and local governments, non-governmental actors, individuals, and businesses to take in order to move millions of Americans from poverty to prosperity.

1. Raise and index the minimum wage to half the average hourly wage. At $5.15, the federal minimum wage is at its lowest level in real terms since 1956. The federal minimum wage was once 50 percent of the average wage, but is now 30 percent of that wage. Congress should restore the minimum wage to 50 percent of the average wage, about $8.40 an hour in 2006. Doing so would help over 4.5 million poor workers and nearly 9 million other low-income workers.

2. Expand the Earned Income Tax Credit and Child Tax Credit. As an earnings supplement for low-income working families, the EITC raises incomes and helps families build assets. The Child Tax Credit provides a tax credit of up to $1,000 per child, but provides no help to the poorest families. We recommend tripling the EITC for childless workers, eliminating the marriage penalty by disregarding half of the lower-earning spouse's wages if doing so would result in an increased EITC for the family, and expanding help to larger working families. We recommend making the Child Tax Credit available to all low- and moderate-income families. Doing so would move 2 million children and 1 million parents out of poverty.

3. Promote unionization by enacting the Employee Free Choice Act. The Employee Free Choice Act would require employers to recognize a union after a majority of workers signs cards authorizing union representation and establish stronger penalties for violations of employee rights. The increased union representation made possible by the Act would lead to better jobs and less poverty for American workers.

4. Guarantee child care assistance to low-income families and promote early education for all. We propose that the federal and state governments guarantee child care help to families with incomes below about $40,000 a year, with expanded tax help to higher-earning families. At the same time, states should be encouraged to improve the quality of early education and broaden access to early education for all children. Our child care expansion would raise employment among low-income parents and help nearly 3 million parents and children escape poverty.

5. Create 2 million new "opportunity" housing vouchers and promote equitable development in and around central cities. Nearly 8 million Americans live in neighborhoods of concentrated poverty where at least 40 percent of residents are poor.

Getting an Education and a Job

Our nation should seek to end concentrated poverty and economic segregation, and promote regional equity and inner-city revitalization. We propose that over the next 10 years the federal government fund 2 million new "opportunity vouchers," designed to help people live in opportunity-rich areas. Any new affordable housing should be in communities with employment opportunities and high-quality public services or in gentrifying communities. These housing policies should be part of a broader effort to pursue equitable development strategies in regional and local planning efforts, including efforts to improve schools, create affordable housing, assure physical security, and enhance neighborhood amenities.

6. Connect disadvantaged and disconnected youth with school and work. About 1.7 million poor youth ages 16 to 24 were both out of school and out of work in 2005. We recommend that the federal government restore Youth Opportunity Grants to help the most disadvantaged communities and expand funding for effective and promising youth programs—with the goal of reaching 600,000 poor disadvantaged youth through these efforts. We propose a new Upward Pathway program to offer low-income youth opportunities to participate in service and training in fields that are in high demand and provide needed public services.

7. Simplify and expand Pell Grants and make higher education accessible to residents of each state. Low-income youth are much less likely to attend college than their higher-income peers, even among those of comparable abilities. Pell Grants play a crucial role for lower-income students. We propose to simplify the Pell Grant application process, gradually raise Pell Grants to reach 70 percent of the average costs of attending a four-year public institution, and encourage institutions to do more to raise student completion rates. As the federal government does its part, states should develop strategies to make post-secondary education affordable for all residents, following promising models already underway in a number of states.

8. Help former prisoners find stable employment and reintegrate into their communities. The United States has the highest incarceration rate in the world. We urge Congress

U.S. Antipoverty Programs Help Only Some Groups

The nation's most potent income-security policies are for the elderly. The combination of Social Security, SSI [Supplemental Security Income] food stamps, and other programs reduced the overall number of seniors living in poverty in 2003 by 14 million (more than 80 percent), and lifted the disposable income of those remaining in poverty from an average of just 8 percent of the poverty line to 62 percent of the poverty line. In addition, Medicare and Medicaid combine to provide health insurance for virtually all of the 35 million Americans age 65 and older. . . .

Public benefits also substantially reduce the amount and severity of poverty for families with children, although not nearly to the same degree as they do for seniors. Government benefits lifted nearly one of every three otherwise-poor children above the poverty line in 2003. For millions of other poor children, poverty was made less severe than it otherwise would have been. . . .

The U.S. safety net is weakest for two other groups—immigrants and non-elderly individuals without children. For immigrant families, eligibility for safety-net programs ranging from food stamps to medical assistance was sharply restricted in the mid-1990s. These cuts have been restored only partially in the years since then. In 2002, low-income people in families headed by an immigrant were only half as likely as Americans overall to have their family income lifted above the poverty line by public benefits. . . .

Arloc Sherman,
Center on Budget and Policy Priorities,
August 17, 2005.

to pass the Second Chance Act, which will support successful models for reintegrating ex-offenders into their communities through job training and education opportunities, drug and mental health treatment, housing and other necessary services. Every state should establish an Office of Reentry Policy, which will oversee statewide reentry efforts and partner with local reentry commissions.

Help the Poor Who Cannot Work

9. Ensure equity for low-wage workers in the Unemployment Insurance system.

Only about 35 percent of the unemployed, and a smaller share of unemployed low-wage workers, receive unemployment insurance benefits. We recommend that states (with federal help) reform "monetary eligibility" rules that screen out low-wage workers, broaden eligibility for part-time workers and workers who have lost employment as a result of compelling family circumstances, and allow unemployed workers to use periods of unemployment as a time to upgrade their skills and qualifications.

10. Modernize means-tested benefits programs to develop a coordinated system that helps workers and families. A well-functioning safety net should help people get into or return to work and ensure a decent level of living for those who cannot work or are temporarily between jobs. Our current system fails to do so. We recommend that governments at all levels simplify and improve benefits access for working families and improve services to individuals with disabilities. The Food Stamp Program should be strengthened to improve benefits, eligibility, and access, and the Temporary Assistance for Needy Families Program should be reformed to strengthen its focus on helping needy families find sustainable employment.

11. Reduce the high costs of being poor and increase access to financial services. Despite having less income, lower-income families often pay more than middle- and high-income families for the same consumer products. We recommend that the federal and state governments address the home mortgage foreclosure crisis through expanded mortgage assistance programs and by new federal legislation to curb unscrupulous practices. And we propose that the federal government establish a $50 million Financial Fairness Innovation Fund to support state efforts to broaden access to mainstream goods and financial services in predominantly low-income communities.

12. Expand and simplify the Saver's Credit to encourage saving for education, homeownership, and retirement. For many families, saving for purposes such as education, a home, or a small business is key to making economic progress. We propose that the federal "Saver's Credit" be reformed to make it fully refundable. This credit should also be broadened to apply to other appropriate savings vehicles intended to foster asset accumulation, with consideration given to including individual development accounts, children's saving accounts, and college savings plans.

We believe these recommendations will cut poverty in half. The Urban Institute, which modeled the implementation of one set of our recommendations (using a methodology drawn from recommendations of a National Academy of Sciences expert panel), estimates that four of our steps would reduce poverty by 26 percent, bringing us more than halfway toward our goal. Among their findings:

The Benefits Are Worth the Costs

Taken together, our minimum wage, EITC, child credit, and child care recommendations would reduce poverty by 26 percent. This would mean over 9 million fewer people in poverty and a national poverty rate of 9.1 percent—the lowest in recorded U.S. history.

The racial poverty gap would be narrowed. White poverty would fall from 8.7 percent to 7.0 percent. Poverty among African Americans would fall from 21.4 percent to 15.6 percent. Hispanic poverty would fall from 21.4 percent to 12.9 percent and poverty for all others would fall from 12.7 percent to 10.3 percent.

Child poverty and extreme poverty would both fall. Child poverty would drop by 41 percent. The number of people in extreme poverty would fall by over 2 million.

Millions of low- and moderate-income families would benefit. Almost half of the benefits would help low- and moderate-income families.

The combined cost of our principal recommendations is in the range of $90 billion a year—a significant cost but one that is necessary and could be readily funded through a fairer tax system. An additional $90 billion in annual spending would represent about 0.8 percent of the nation's gross domestic product, which is a fraction of the money spent on tax changes that benefited primarily the wealthy in recent years. Consider that:

> The current annual costs of the tax cuts enacted by Congress in 2001 and 2003 are in the range of $400 billion a year.

> In 2008 alone the value of the tax cuts to households with incomes exceeding $200,000 a year is projected to be $100 billion.

Our recommendations could be fully paid for simply by bringing better balance to the federal tax system and recouping part of what has been lost by the excessive tax cuts of recent years. We recognize that serious action has serious costs, but the challenge before the nation is not whether we can afford to act, but rather that we must decide to act. What would it mean to accomplish a 50-percent reduction in poverty? In concrete terms, it would mean that nearly 20 million fewer Americans would be living in poverty. It would mean more working Americans, dramatically fewer working people in poverty, stronger, more vibrant communities, and millions of children beginning their lives with vastly more opportunity than they have today. It would mean a healthier population, less crime, more economic growth, a more capable workforce, a more competitive nation, and a major decline in the racial inequities and disparities that have plagued our nation. I think this is a vision of society worth fighting for. Reducing poverty is the right thing to do and critical for the success of our nation and our people.

"It was the stick of welfare reform that induced mothers to leave welfare for work; it was the carrot of work-support benefits . . . that led to substantial reductions in poverty."

Poverty Has Been Reduced by Restricting Government Programs

Ron Haskins and Isabel Sawhill

Developmental psychologist Ron Haskins and economist Isabel Sawhill are senior fellows and codirectors of the Center on Children and Families at the Washington, DC, think tank the Brookings Institution. In the following viewpoint, Haskins and Sawhill argue that reducing poverty depends not on economic growth but on social engineering, which they describe in terms of "carrots" and "sticks"—that is, on incentives that reward work and responsible behavior and discourage dependence on government handouts. According to Haskins and Sawhill, reducing or terminating cash welfare payments to recipients who did not meet work requirements, and limiting benefits to five years, were "sticks" that prodded millions of people out of poverty in the mid-1990s, and similar principles should underlie policies to reduce the poverty rate today.

As you read, consider the following questions:

1. Why do Haskins and Sawhill dispute President John F. Kennedy's maxim that "a rising tide lifts all boats."

2. How much did federal and state spending on poverty programs increase between 1968 and 2004, according to the authors?

3. What six ideas do the authors say are better ways to reduce poverty than by increasing government welfare benefits?

In the last decade, we have seen that an effective approach to reducing poverty requires changes in personal behavior as well as government support. Further, we have learned that by judiciously applying policies that demand and then reward good behavior—what might be called carrots-and-sticks policies—we can induce and maintain the behavior that leads to reduced poverty. Reviewing the record of the past decade suggests the principles that should guide future efforts.

During the 1960s, child poverty fell by more than half, to 14 percent. In the subsequent three decades, however, child poverty drifted upward in an uneven pattern, never again reaching the low level achieved in 1969. This is a surprising and discouraging record.

A major cause of the huge decline in poverty of the 1960s was an economy that grew 35 percent in per capita gross domestic product, giving rise to President [John F.] Kennedy's famous observation that "a rising tide lifts all boats." Although the American economy has grown at a more stately pace since the 1960s, each subsequent decade has nonetheless seen substantial growth of more than 20 percent in per capita GDP [gross domestic product]—plenty of raw material, one would think, to continue the poverty reduction that distinguished the '60s. But the 24 percent GDP growth of the 1970s saw poverty fall by a mere 5 percent, and the 23 percent GDP growth of the '80s saw poverty actually *increase* by 12 percent. Clearly, a rising tide was not lifting all boats. The second half of the '90s, however, once again saw strong economic growth accompanied by the fastest and deepest decline in child poverty since the '60s.

Why Did Poverty Decline?

Three trends tell us a lot about the causes of poverty and show us why a growing economy has not been more effective in reducing it. First, growth of wages at the bottom of the distribution (the 10th percentile) declined during the 1980s and the first half of the '90s, rising again only after 1996.

High Employment. Stagnant or falling wages at the bottom of the distribution make reducing poverty difficult. By contrast, tight labor markets, as signaled by low unemployment rates, contribute to both rising wages and falling poverty rates.

Consider the record: Wages rose and poverty fell during the 1960s, when unemployment averaged 4.8 percent and fell as low as 3.5 percent. But as wages fell or were stagnant during the '70s and '80s, when unemployment skyrocketed to average 6.2 percent and 7.3 percent, respectively, poverty rose or was stagnant. Only when tight labor markets returned after the mid-'90s—when unemployment fell to an average of 4.8 percent between 1995 and 2000—did wages once again rise and poverty fall. Mere economic growth will not necessarily lead to reduced poverty rates. Apparently, tight labor markets accompanied by rising wages are required to effectively fight poverty.

Family Factors. A second factor putting substantial upward pressure on poverty was changes in family composition. The poverty rate for mother-headed families is usually four or five times the rate for married-couple families. So, other things being equal, any rise in the share of children living in female-headed families will increase poverty.

Beginning in the 1960s, Americans perfected every known method of casting children into single-parent families. Marriage rates fell, divorce rates increased until the 1980s, and non-marital birth rates exploded until a third of all babies (and nearly 70 percent of black babies) were born outside marriage. As a result, between 1970 and 2004, the percentage of children living in a female-headed family increased from 12 percent to 28 percent. It's hard to fight poverty when more and more children are in families of the type that are most likely to be poor.

Education. Poor educational achievement is a third reason poverty has been stagnant. Education has always been important in accounting for economic success, but most analysts agree that recent decades—because of globalization, technological change, and trade—have seen increased payoff to education. One of the most important changes in the American economy for those interested in fighting poverty is the decline of high-paying jobs suited to workers with a high-school education or less. Workers without a high-school diploma are twice as likely to be poor as those with one, and three times as likely to be poor as workers with some college education. The Educational Testing Service estimates that nearly one-third of students drop out of school before graduating. Moreover, despite waves of educational reform, the reading and math achievement of students from poor and low-income families has been virtually flat for three decades.

So there are at least three raging rivers against which those who would fight poverty must struggle: low wages, the rise of single-parent families, and lousy education. To offset these currents, the nation has spent an increasing amount of money on government programs to fight poverty. Between 1968 and 2004, the total of inflation-adjusted federal and state spending on means-tested programs (those that specify an income level

Government Interference Creates Poverty

Just as the wage rates of workers, especially the lowest paid, could be substantially increased by the reduction of government interference, so too the prices paid by all workers could be substantially reduced by the reduction of government interference. . . .

There is no good reason, for example, for the price of oil to be over $50 a barrel and rising. In a free market, that is, a market not hampered by such things as regulations driven by environmentalist hysteria and a valuation of human well-being below that of caribou, there would be a substantially increased supply of oil from Alaska. There would also be an increased supply from offshore fields in the Gulf of Mexico and off the coast of California. And added to this would undoubtedly be major increases in the supply of oil from other parts of the United States, now ruled off limits to exploration and development because they have been set aside as wildlife preserves or wilderness areas. These increases in supply would substantially reduce the price of oil.

The price of oil would also be reduced by removing the obstacles in the way of the production of atomic power and the strip mining of coal. Increased supplies of atomic power and coal would serve to reduce the demand for oil and thus its price. The price of food could be substantially reduced by the abolition of government farm subsidies.

The cost of housing could be reduced by the abolition of zoning laws and all other government interference serving to make land artificially scarce, such as the restrictions on land use imposed by the California Coastal Commission. It could be reduced by the liberalization of government mandated building and safety codes and by the withdrawal of government support for construction unions. . . .

George Reisman, Mises Institute, October 13, 2004.

above which individuals or families cannot qualify for benefits) increased from $89 billion to $585 billion—all without reducing poverty below its late-1960s level.

The net impact of these factors—economic growth, wages, family composition, education, and government spending—is high child-poverty rates. It is especially notable that the three factors over which individuals have full or partial control—work, family composition, and education—were either stable or moved in the wrong direction. Until recently, millions of Americans failed to work, many languishing on welfare. Millions also decided to have children outside marriage, to avoid marriage, or to divorce. And millions of young people refused to apply themselves during their school years, eventually either dropping out of school or graduating with low reading and math skills.

The Role of Welfare Reform

Yet the mid-1990s saw a dramatic example of how public policy can both help individuals improve their choices and reward them for doing so, namely the 1996 welfare-reform law, passed on a huge bipartisan vote in Congress and signed by Democratic President Bill Clinton. Perhaps the law's single most notable feature was that it made cash welfare contingent on individuals working or preparing for work. Individuals who did not meet work requirements had their cash benefit reduced, and in most states even terminated.

In addition, the law limited federal benefit receipt to five years for any given parent. The work requirements, reduction of benefits for those who did not work, and five-year time limit all served as sticks that encouraged or forced parents on welfare to work. Much to everyone's surprise, mothers went to work by the hundreds of thousands, and the welfare rolls declined by more than 60 percent, far more than ever before. But most important, poverty among children in single-parent families fell by 30 percent, reaching its lowest level ever. Not surprisingly, given the high proportion of black children living in female-headed families, black child poverty also reached its lowest level ever.

Raising Rewards of Work

Government-imposed work requirements were an important part of this welcome decline in child poverty. But work is only half the picture. Most welfare mothers, who typically can qualify for jobs paying about $8 per hour, were not able to earn enough money to bring their families out of poverty. Realizing that financial payoffs to work were an important part of helping low-income families, federal and state governments, over a period of more than two decades, created and expanded programs specifically designed to help low-income working families. These included Medicaid health insurance, child care, food stamps, and above all, the Earned Income Tax Credit (EITC), a taxpayer-provided wage subsidy that could give working parents up to $4,000 in cash (in 1996).

Census Bureau data for children living with their single mothers, present a clear picture of why this new system of earnings from increased work effort supplemented by benefits from work-support programs led to such a dramatic reduction in child poverty.... Increased work by mothers between 1990 and '99 led to a huge 11 percentage point reduction in poverty. When government cash and in-kind benefits other than those delivered through the tax code are added, poverty falls 13 percentage points in 1990. But poverty also falls by 9 percentage points in 1999, demonstrating that working families are receiving work-support benefits to supplement their earnings to further reduce market poverty. Adding tax benefits, primarily the EITC does not reduce poverty at all in 1990, but reduces it another 5 percentage points in 1999. The combination of work and work supports reduces poverty a full 12 percentage points—or by about 4.5 million people—more in 1999 than in 1990. It was the stick of welfare reform that induced mothers to leave welfare for work; it was the carrot of work-support benefits that supplemented the mothers' earnings and led to substantial reductions in poverty.

There are lots of good ideas for further reductions in poverty—improving and expanding preschool education; improving the public schools, especially for students from poor families; reducing nonmarital births; increasing marriage rates; encouraging savings; and helping poor young men improve their earnings—but the decline of poverty among female-headed families in the 1990s illustrates the principles that should guide the nation's efforts. The first is that individuals must change their behavior—or the nation will not be able to substantially reduce poverty. The second is that policy-makers should seek out policies that encourage or demand responsible behavior, and then use public dollars to reward it.

| *"Low tax rates are a significant factor in ... poverty reduction."*

Tax Cuts Reduce Poverty

Matthew Ladner

Matthew Ladner is vice president for research at the Goldwater Institute, a public policy organization in Phoenix, Arizona. In 2006 Ladner coauthored a study of the relationship between U.S. state tax rates and poverty rates. In the following viewpoint, he argues a cause-and-effect relationship between the two variables: Between 1990 and 2000, the states with the lowest tax rates experienced the greatest reduction in poverty, and the states with the highest taxes also had the highest poor populations.

As you read, consider the following questions:

1. What was the average poverty reduction in the ten states with the lowest tax burdens, according to Ladner?

2. Why does Ladner dismiss illegal immigration as a cause of high poverty rates in California?

3. How do lower taxes spur economic growth, according to the author?

When the US government ended "welfare as we know it" in 1996, it handed responsibility for reform to the states. In so doing, it also created a real-world test of two competing economic strategies used to fight poverty. The results are in and the lessons are clear: Low tax rates lift up the lives of America's poor.

Many people argue that government can reduce poverty by "redistributing" wealth through progressive taxation—imposing higher tax rates on higher income brackets—and through more government spending.

Most economists, however, say the best way to reduce poverty is through stronger economic growth. Growth means more jobs, a surefire antipoverty plan. Building a strong economy means keeping taxes and government spending low.

A study published [in November 2006] by the Goldwater Institute, "How to Win the War on Poverty: An Analysis of State Poverty Trends," tests these different theories by examining state poverty rates from 1990 to 2000.

Nationwide, states took great strides in reducing both general and childhood poverty. Poverty fell by 5.3 percent and childhood poverty by 9.4 percent. Some states, however, reduced poverty much more than others, while some states suffered large increases.

Take Colorado. It reduced its childhood poverty rate by almost 27 percent. Meanwhile, Rhode Island's childhood poverty rate increased by almost the same amount. What accounts for those differences?

Using data from the Census Bureau, the report found that states with the lowest tax rates enjoyed sizable decreases in poverty. For example, the 10 states with the lowest total state and local tax burdens saw an average poverty reduction of 13 percent—two times better than the national average. The 10 highest-tax states, meanwhile, suffered an average increase in poverty of 3 percent.

Cut Both Taxes and Spending to Reduce Poverty

The relative success of low-tax states in reducing poverty is somewhat unsurprising. Sure, less taxation spurs the economy, thus creating jobs and economic growth. But, what about spending? [A 2007 Rio Grande Foundation study] compared the 10 states with the lowest per-capita spending during the 1990s with the top 10 states in per capita spending. In the low-spending states, overall poverty rates declined by a robust 8.42% while the big-spenders not only failed to reduce poverty rates, but they actually suffered an increase in poverty rates of 7.6%.

Paul J. Gessing, Human Events, *April 5, 2007.*

High Taxes Mean Increases in Poverty

Some high-tax states, such as California, Hawaii, and New York, suffered catastrophic increases in poverty. As California began to reject the low-tax legacy of the [Ronald] Reagan governorship, the state's poverty rate jumped 13 percent in the 1990s.

Some will be quick to dismiss this as a consequence of illegal immigration. But lower-tax border states such as Arizona and Texas had substantial declines in poverty while also experiencing large increases in immigration.

In fact, California's high taxation has been so damaging to the economy that another increase like the one in the 1990s would result in poverty exceeding Mississippi's by 2010.

When a state has a low tax burden, economic growth is stronger. Economic growth delivers more job creation and higher per capita and median family incomes. Economic growth is a powerful means to pull people out of poverty.

Although some policymakers justify high taxes for the sake of the poor, the data show that higher taxes and related spending do little to reduce poverty rates. Rather, states with healthy economic climates have much more success in lifting people out of poverty.

The causes of, and solutions to, poverty are complex, but one policy is clear: Low tax rates are a significant factor in achieving the universal goal of poverty reduction.

"*Drastic reductions in social spending are paired with a package of more tax cuts for the wealthy.*"

Tax Cuts Hurt the Poor

National Organization for Women

The National Organization for Women (NOW), founded in 1966 and headquartered in Washington, DC, is an activist feminist organization of a half million members whose primary issues are pro-choice reproductive rights, domestic violence, and racial and sex discrimination. In the following viewpoint, NOW condemns the George W. Bush administration's tax and budget cuts as discriminatory and misleading—portrayed as necessary to aid post-Hurricane Katrina recovery but in fact benefiting the rich at the expense of poor families, many headed by single women. Reductions in federal spending forced by tax cuts have targeted social programs, NOW argues, including child-care assistance, disability payments, student loans, and Medicaid, which only widens the gap between the haves and have-nots in American society, it maintains.

National Organization for Women, "Reprehensible Budget Slashes Human Needs Programs to Pay for Tax Cuts for the Rich," *National NOW Times*, Spring 2006. Reproduced by permission.

As you read, consider the following questions:

1. How have federal child-care assistance programs been affected by spending cuts necessitated by tax cuts, according to NOW?
2. How have tax cuts affected the Medicaid health-care program, in the author's view?
3. How much does NOW estimate tax breaks that went into effect in January 2006 will cost the U.S. Treasury over the next ten years?

On Feb. 1 [2006], the House of Representatives narrowly approved the 2006 budget reconciliation bill (S. 1932) that cuts nearly $40 billion over five years from scores of critically important federal programs, including Medicaid, child support enforcement, disability assistance, child care for poor families, welfare funding and student loan programs. These drastic reductions in social spending are paired with a package of more tax cuts for the wealthy that may lead to as much as $90 billion in lost revenues.

"Republican budgeteers have targeted these disgraceful cuts at the most vulnerable members of society," said National Organization for Women President Kim Gandy. "Those most affected by this mean-spirited budget bill will be poor women and children—and hard working, struggling families will be hurt as well."

Republican leaders earlier suggested that these reductions in federal spending were needed to pay for the cost of Katrina recovery, but it is now clear that the cuts will instead offset revenues lost because of new and extended tax cuts, primarily benefiting the already-wealthy and the highest income earners.

Drastic Cuts in Antipoverty Programs

Child Care Assistance Slashed. Only $1 billion is provided for child care programs for welfare beneficiaries even though modest estimates show that more than $7 billion would be needed to aid parents who, under this legislation, will also be forced to work longer hours. It is estimated that by 2010, some 255,000 additional children in low-income working families will have been denied child care aid.

Tougher Welfare Work Requirements. Because states will have to meet higher work participation requirements under the reauthorized Temporary Assistance to Needy Families (TANF) welfare program, they will likely have to adopt stricter policies and deny aid to more poor families. The legislation does not provide additional funds to states to meet these new and expensive requirements, and actually provides incentives to states to exclude two-parent families from TANF.

Child Support Collections Cut. Federal monies for child support enforcement will be deeply cut, translating to a projected loss of $24 billion in child support over the next ten years, according to the Congressional Budget Office. Better enforcement in recent years has led to higher collections for thousands of low- and moderate income families. In many instances, the receipt of child support payments is essential to sustaining a low-income family and helping them avoid public assistance.

Foster Care Relatives Denied Help. Foster care funding assistance for grandparents and other relatives will no longer be available in certain states; many foster care programs are already seriously under-funded and there are insufficient numbers of families in most states willing to care for foster children.

Disability Benefits Delayed. People with disabilities will have to wait as long as a year to receive benefits due to a new restriction imposed by this budget. Many individuals with disabilities are in desperate financial straits and already must wait for many months to become eligible under the Social Security Supplemental Security Income (SSI) program.

Student Loans Will Cost More. Funding for student loans will be slashed by $12.7 billion over the next five years; the reductions are produced by increasing interest rates and hiking fees paid by students and parents. These changes will affect low- and moderate-income families struggling to meet ever-increasing costs of a college education (40 percent rise over last five years) and could amount to as much as $3,000 more in interest payments per student.

Reductions in Health Care for the Poor

Medicaid May Become Unaffordable. Increases in Medicaid co-payments and premiums plus reductions in benefits will total $29 billion over the next ten years, according to the Congressional Budget Office. Recipients, the majority of whom are poor and elderly women and children, will have to meet much higher premiums and co-payments for health care, and states will be allowed to cut back on Medicaid services. These and other changes will mean that many low-income persons will simply not be able to afford services.

Medicaid Changes Are Draconian. It is important to note that the changes to Medicaid will mean that millions of low-income children could lose coverage for critical health care services, like payment for eyeglasses, hearing aids, speech therapy, crutches, and other medically necessary treatments that are often unaffordable to low-income parents. In addition, the legislation will make it more difficult to qualify for long-term care coverage under Medicaid—a roadblock to the only source of care for thousands of low-income elderly and disabled women. Millions of taxpayer dollars are being allocated for erectile dysfunction drugs, while vital services for the elderly, disabled and children are being dramatically reduced. In addition, a new mandate for proof of citizenship before receiving eligibility under Medicaid will mean that between three and five million U.S. citizens could see their Medicaid coverage jeopardized, according to a recent survey conducted by the Center on Budget and Policy Priorities. No exceptions will be made for persons having lost documentation due to homelessness (or hurricanes) or for persons with serious mental or physical disabilities. About 49 million U.S.-born citizens and two million naturalized citizens will now be required to produce proof of citizenship.

For the first time in the history of Medicaid, states can deny contraception and family planning services to poor women. Required under all previous versions of Medicaid, provision of both family planning services and contraception are essential to the health of Medicaid recipients. States can now opt out of providing these services, undermining the health of millions of the nation's poorest. Constraining access to contraception will undoubtedly increase unintended pregnancies, the public costs of which far outstrip the cost savings of limiting contraception.

Fatherhood and Marriage Programs Funded. This legislation includes up to $50 million annually to fund questionable fatherhood programs. These funds have been taken from other seriously under-funded TANF programs and NOW suspects that some of those monies will end up with extremist "fathers' rights" groups. The authorized total would be $150 million annually for both fatherhood and marriage promotion initiatives; all states will be mandated under this bill to establish marriage promotion programs and to meet numerical performance objectives. NOW regards marriage promotion efforts targeting low-income women as potentially coercive, discriminatory and an invasion of privacy.

Tax Cuts Force Spending Cuts

A separate bill (H.R. 4297) that will reduce taxes by $56 billion—mostly for the super-rich through an extension of reduced taxes on capital gains and dividend income—was adopted by the House on Dec. 8 [2005] by a vote of 234–197. Three similar measures subsequently passed the House, including a $31 billion, one-year extension provision limiting the Alternative Minimum Tax; $7 billion in tax incentives for

Poor Lose More than They Gain from Tax Cuts

The Bush administration and Congress have scaled back programs that aid the poor to help pay for $600 billion in tax breaks that went primarily to those who earn more than $288,800 a year.

The affected programs—job training, housing, higher education and an array of social services—provide safety nets for the poor. Many programs are critical elements in welfare-to-work initiatives and were already badly underfunded. . . .

The loss of services cost many poor Americans more money than they saved from the tax cuts.

In many cases, the poorest lost services and got no tax cut at all.

The analysis of the three Bush tax cuts is based in part on estimates by the Center on Budget and Policy Priorities, using data from the nonpartisan Congressional Budget Office.

The poorest 20 percent of workers, who earn on average $16,600 annually, will get a tax break of $250 [in 2004], which is less than 2 percent of their income. That amounts to about 68 cents a day.

By comparison, the richest 1 percent, with average incomes topping $1.1 million, will receive $78,460 in tax cuts [in 2004]. That is nearly 7 percent of their income.

Melvin Claxton and Ronald J. Hansen,
Detroit News, *September 26, 2004.*

Gulf Coast hurricane-damaged states; and a package of five small tax provisions not included in the larger reconciliation package. The whopping total will be a loss of $90 billion over the next five years!

Furthermore, the two new tax breaks which went into effect January 1, 2006, will cost the Treasury almost $150 billion over the next ten years. These pertain to limitations on the value of the personal exemptions and itemized deductions that high income earners can take. Most of the monetary gains will go to households with incomes above $1 million annually, according to the Center on Budget and Policy Priorities.

A new state-level study by the Center on Budget and Policy Priorities and by Economic Policy Institute finds that the gap between the highest-income families and poor and middle-income families grew significantly between the early 1980s and the early 2000s. Though income inequality declined briefly following the stock and high tech bubble burst of 2000, inequality began growing again in 2003. By contrast—and a surprise to no one—the incomes of the nation's richest families have climbed substantially over the past two decades, while middle- and lower-income families have seen only moderate increases. The analysis is based on adjusted Census income data and more information is available online.

While Katrina-related tax reductions of $7.8 billion were adopted by both houses and signed into law on Dec. 22 [2005] most of the dispossessed and those harmed by the hurricane and flooding will be equally hurt by the cruel budget cuts to the very programs that will help the human recovery effort.

"Hurricane Katrina illuminated the stark differences between the rich and the poor in this country," Gandy said. "Rather than helping to eliminate the gaps, these tax reductions and program cuts will only widen them. The members of Congress who vote for these cuts are trading in their integrity and compassion to benefit the rich."

> "Make the grant large enough so that the poor won't be poor. . . . We're rich enough to do it."

Replace Antipoverty Programs with Annual Cash Grants for Every Adult American

Charles A. Murray

Political scientist Charles Murray is W.H. Brady Scholar at the American Enterprise Institute, a conservative think tank in Washington, DC, and the coauthor of The Bell Curve, *a controversial examination of intelligence and class structure in American life. In 2006 Murray again stirred controversy with the publication of* In Our Hands: A Plan to Replace the Welfare State, *in which he presented a radical proposal to scrap existing social welfare programs (including Social Security and Medicare) and instead pay every American aged eighteen and older ten thousand dollars annually for life, as a solution to poverty. In the following viewpoint, Murray explains his proposal, called "the Plan," defends its costs, and predicts the wholesale reform of the existing benefits network as inevitable.*

As you read, consider the following questions:

1. What percentage of gross domestic product is consumed by Social Security, Medicare, and Medicaid today, and what will be the percentage in 2050 under the current system, according to Murray?

2. Under Murray's Plan, how would a twenty-one-year-old man be able to avoid poverty in retirement?

3. How does the Plan ensure personal accountability (so that cash payments are not simply spent and wasted), in Murray's view?

This much is certain: The welfare state as we know it cannot survive. No serious student of entitlements thinks that we can let federal spending on Social Security, Medicare and Medicaid rise from its current 9% of gross domestic product [GDP] to the 28% of GDP that it will consume in 2050 if past growth rates continue. The problems facing transfer programs for the poor are less dramatic but, in the long term, no less daunting; the falling value of a strong back and the rising value of brains will eventually create a class society making a mockery of America's ideals unless we come up with something more creative than anything that the current welfare system has to offer. . . .

Scrap the Existing Structure

The place to start is a blindingly obvious economic reality that no one seems to notice: This country is awash in money. America is so wealthy that enabling everyone to have a decent standard of living is easy. We cannot do it by fiddling with the entitlement and welfare systems—they constitute a Gordian Knot that cannot be untied. But we can cut the knot. We can scrap the structure of the welfare state.

Instead of sending taxes to Washington, straining them through bureaucracies and converting what remains into a muddle of services, subsidies, in-kind support and cash hedged with restrictions and exceptions, just collect the taxes, divide them up, and send the money back in cash grants to all American adults. Make the grant large enough so that the poor won't be poor, everyone will have enough for a comfortable retirement, and everyone will be able to afford health care. We're rich enough to do it.

A Better Plan

Consider retirement. Let's say that we have a 21-year-old man before us who, for whatever reasons, will be unable to accumulate his own retirement fund. We accumulate it for him through a yearly contribution for 45 years until he retires at age 66. We can afford to contribute $2,000 a year and invest it in an index-based stock fund. What is the least he can expect to have when he retires? We are ridiculously conservative, so we first identify the worst compound average growth rate, using constant dollars, for any 45-year period in the history of the stock market (4.3% from 1887–1932). We then assume our 21-year-old will be the unluckiest investor in American history and get just a 4.0% average return. At the end of the 45-year period, he will have about $253,000, with which he could purchase an annuity worth about $20,500 a year.

That's with just a $2,000 annual contribution, equivalent to the Social Security taxes [FICA] the government gets for a person making only $16,129 a year. The government gets more than twice that amount from someone earning the median income, and more than five times that amount from the millions of people who pay the maximum FICA tax. Giving everyone access to a comfortable retirement income is easy for a country as rich as the U.S.—if we don't insist on doing it through the structure of the welfare state.

Health care is more complicated in its details, but not in its logic. We do not wait until our 21-year-old is 65 and then start paying for his health care. Instead, we go to a health insurance company and tell it that we're prepared to start paying a constant premium now for the rest of the 21-year-old's life. Given that kind of offer, the health insurance company can sell us a health care policy that covers the essentials for somewhere around $3,000. It can be so inexpensive for the same reason that life insurance companies can sell generous life insurance cheaply if people buy it when they're young—the insurance company makes a lot of money from the annual payments before eventually having to write the big benefit checks. Providing access to basic medical care for everyone is easy for a country as rich as the U.S.—if we don't insist on doing it through the structure of the welfare state.

There are many ways of turning these economic potentials into a working system. The one I have devised—I call it simply "the Plan" for want of a catchier label—makes a $10,000 annual grant to all American citizens who are not incarcerated, beginning at age 21, of which $3,000 a year must be used for health care. Everyone gets a monthly check, deposited electronically to a bank account. If we implemented the Plan tomorrow, it would cost about $355 billion more than the current system. The projected costs of the Plan cross the projected costs of the current system in 2011. By 2020, the Plan would cost about half a trillion dollars less per year than conservative projections of the cost of the current system. By 2028, that difference would be a trillion dollars per year. . . .

Individual Purpose and Responsibility

Do we want a system in which the government divests itself of responsibility for the human needs that gave rise to the welfare state in the first place? I think the reasons for answering "yes" go far beyond the Plan's effects on poverty, retirement and health care. Those issues affect comparatively small minorities of the population. The more profound problem facing the world's most advanced societies is how their peoples are to live meaningful lives in an age of plenty and security.

Not Just a Free-for-All

It is to [Charles] Murray's great credit that—despite his libertarian, let-them-fend-for-themselves instincts—he's built human imperfection into his Plan. . . .

For example, he'd require everyone to use part of their grant to buy health insurance—gritting his teeth, he even admits he'd have the government withhold those monies (probably around $250/month) from the monthly paychecks.

And how does he figure $250/month? [Murray] wants to "legally obligate medical insurers to treat the entire population as a single pool," and that would probably run to $3,000 per person per year. (At the same time, Murray wants to reform tort law so low-cost medical clinics could open their doors throughout the land and be immune from esoteric lawsuits. . . .

Another way Murray addresses human imperfection is by (grudgingly) conceding that "the Plan could be modified to stipulate that some percentage of the grant be deposited in a retirement account of diversified stocks and bonds."

It's not his first choice—he doesn't want to "reduce the ability of people to pursue their dreams for how to live their lives." But he reluctantly concedes that mandatory retirement accounts would in fact keep some people (generally the neediest) from having to retire on the $10,000/year grant alone.

Mark Satin,
Radical Middle Newsletter,
April 15, 2006.

Throughout history until a few decades ago, the meaning of life for almost everyone was linked to the challenge of simple survival. Staying alive required being a contributing part of a community. Staying alive required forming a family and having children to care for you in your old age. The knowledge that sudden death could happen at any moment required attention to spiritual issues. Doing all those things provided deep satisfactions that went beyond survival.

Life in an age of plenty and security requires none of those things. For the great majority of people living in advanced societies, it is easily possible to go through life accompanied by social companions and serial sex partners, having a good time, and dying in old age with no reason to think that one has done anything significant.

If you believe that's all there is—that the purpose of life is to while away the time as pleasantly as possible—then it is reasonable to think that the purpose of government should be to enable people to do so with as little effort as possible. But if you agree with me that to live a human life can have transcendental meaning, then we need to think about how human existence acquires weight and consequence.

For many . . . the focus of that search for meaning is bound up with vocation—for some, the quest to be rich and famous; for others, the quest to excel in a vocation one loves. But it is an option open to only to a lucky minority. For most people—including many older people who in their youths focused on vocation—life acquires meaning through the stuff of life: the elemental events associated with birth, death, growing up, raising children, paying the rent, dealing with adversity, comforting the bereaved, celebrating success, applauding the good and condemning the bad; coping with life as it exists around us in all its richness. The chief defect of the welfare state from this perspective is not that it is ineffectual in making good on its promises (though it is), nor even that it often exacerbates the very problems it is supposed to solve (though it does). The welfare state is pernicious ultimately because it drains too much of the life from life.

What If the Money Is Just Wasted?

The Plan returns the stuff of life to all of us in many ways, but chiefly through its effects on the core institutions of family and community. One key to thinking about how the Plan does so is the universality of the grant. What matters is not just that a lone individual has $10,000 a year, but that everyone has $10,000 a year and everyone knows that everyone else has that resource. Strategies that are not open to an individual are open to a couple; strategies that are not open to a couple are open to an extended family or, for that matter, to half a dozen friends who pool resources; strategies not open to a small group are open to a neighborhood. The aggregate shift in resources from government to people under the Plan is massive, and possibilities for dealing with human needs through family and community are multiplied exponentially.

The Plan confers personal accountability whether the recipient wants it or not, producing cascading secondary and tertiary effects. A person who asks for help because he has frittered away his monthly check will find people and organizations who will help (America has a history of producing such people and organizations in abundance), but that help can come with expectations and demands that are hard to make of a person who has no income stream. Or contemplate the effects of a known income stream on the young man who impregnates his girlfriend. The first-order effect is that he cannot evade child support—the judge knows where his bank account is. The second-order effect is to create expectations that formerly didn't exist. I call it the Doolittle Effect, after Alfred Doolittle in "My Fair Lady." Recall why he had to get to the church on time, [once a poor reprobate, Doolittle gets a job and takes on middle-class responsibilities, including getting married].

Practice Responsibility

The Plan confers responsibility for dealing with human needs on all of us, whether we want it or not. Some will see this as a step backward, thinking that it is better to pay one's taxes, give responsibility to the government and be done with it. I think an alternative outlook is wiser: The Plan does not require us all to become part-time social workers. The nation can afford lots of free riders. But Aristotle was right. Virtue is a habit. Virtue does not flourish in the next generation because we tell our children to be honest, compassionate and generous in the abstract. It flourishes because our children practice honesty, compassion and generosity in the same way that they practice a musical instrument or a sport. That happens best when children grow up in a society in which human needs are not consigned to bureaucracies downtown but are part of life around us, met by people around us.

Simply put, the Plan gives us back the action. Institutions and individuals alike thrive to the extent that they have important jobs to do and know that the responsibility to do them is on their heads. For decades, the welfare state has said to us, "We'll take care of that." As a result, we have watched some of our sources of life's most important satisfactions lose vitality. At the same time, we have learned how incompetent—how helpless—government is when "taking care of that" means dealing with complex human needs. The solution is not to tinker with the welfare state. The solution is to put responsibility for our lives back in our hands—ours as individuals, ours as families, and ours as communities.

> *"You cannot put today's . . . Social Security recipients . . . on a flat annual income of $10,000 and expect to survive."*

Replacing Antipoverty Programs with Cash Grants Is Unworkable

Clive Crook

Clive Crook is a senior editor of the Atlantic Monthly, *a columnist for* National Journal, *and a commentator for the* Financial Times. *In the following viewpoint, Crook challenges political scientist Charles Murray's radical proposal to sharply reduce poverty by scrapping existing social welfare programs and simply pay every adult American ten thousand dollars annually for life. Crook says that the plan is impractical and exorbitantly expensive. In particular, he faults Murray for ignoring the fact that implementing the Plan would leave older Americans, who have not had decades to invest their cash payments, totally unprepared to support themselves on ten thousand dollars a year. In general, he says Murray underestimates the costs of the Plan and overestimates human nature.*

As you read, consider the following questions:

1. What costs of the Plan does Crook say Murray fails to consider?

2. Why does the author say Murray's figure of ten thousand dollars per year is too low, even adjusted for inflation over the next fifty years?

3. What fundamental principle of the Plan does Crook say *is* worthy and *should be* a guiding principle in reducing poverty in America?

In our Hands [American Enterprise scholar Charles Murray's plan to replace welfare programs with cash grants] calls for the whole apparatus of the welfare state to be dismantled—not pruned or reformed, but abolished outright. No more Social Security, no more Medicare or Medicaid, no more unemployment benefits. Nothing. These and all such programs that directly transfer income from one group (taxpayers) to others would be not merely terminated but forbidden: Murray calls for a constitutional amendment to that effect. Taking their place—at, Murray says, far lower cost and with vast side benefits for the country's social well-being—would be a payment of $10,000 a year to every American adult. No more poverty, no more welfare state. Simple as that.

Does Murray think it could ever happen? Yes and no. The plan, he agrees, is politically impossible right now. But look ahead, he argues, and it is not just feasible but maybe even inevitable. The welfare state is doomed, not because it causes enormous damage to the social fabric (which, he says, it does) but because it will be financially insupportable. As he wrote in the *Wall Street Journal* on March 22, 2006, "The welfare state as we know it cannot survive. No serious student of entitlements thinks that we can let federal spending on Social Security, Medicare, and Medicaid rise from its current 9 percent of gross domestic product [GDP] to the 28 percent of GDP that it will consume in 2050 if past growth rates continue." . . .

Murray deserves praise for casting his proposal in a concrete form, exposing himself to proper argument and rebuttal. And, in my view at least, many of his larger ideas are right. The main one, to be sure, is extremely attractive: Empower and oblige individuals to take responsibility for themselves and others, not just as a way to confront poverty, but because individual self-determination is the correct organizing principle for society. For many of Murray's critics, that will be the sticking point—but not here. I buy the big idea. It's the details that slow me down.

Murray's Plan Is Unaffordable

Murray is less interested in costs, one surmises, than in social transformation. Yet he insists that his plan is affordable, much more so than the current system, and he goes to some trouble in the book to explain why. As just noted, he aims to motivate his readers by arguing that, in the longer term, the issue of affordability is going to swing the political calculus his way. So it isn't nit-picking or beside the point to question this.

At first blush, the claim that every American adult could be paid $10,000 a year at less cost than the present array of piecemeal welfare payments is indeed startling—even if, as Murray proposes, part of the $10,000 would be clawed back through taxes for Americans earning more than $25,000. Throughout, Murray takes pains to point out that he rests this claim on the least favorable assumptions for the argument he is advancing. But can it really be true? If it is, the idea surely deserves serious consideration.

Unfortunately, Murray is not claiming that it is true straight away. Using his own numbers, switching instantly and comprehensively from the present system of benefits to his plan would leave a shortfall of $355 billion a year—which, at 3 percent of GDP, is a very large sum. His point is that the cost of his plan would grow much more slowly than the projected costs of the welfare state. "I will not bother," he says, "to

What About Poor Children?

If everyone in the world belonged to a single generation, I would say that "the Plan" (as [Charles] Murray calls his proposal) sounds wonderful. But we do not live in such a world. We live in a world with children. And it is poor children who, under the plan, may seriously suffer.

Start with what it costs to raise a child. Each mother would receive $583 a month and health insurance from age 21 till death. That takes care of the Medicare issue. But what about her children? I pay about $400 per month in health-insurance premiums for my family, and my employer matches that amount, a total of almost $10,000 a year. So the cost for parents is remarkably higher than the $3,000 Murray has allotted. And remember, without Medicare, the money has to be stretched to cover health expenses in old age. So it couldn't possibly cover children too. Children are the second most expensive group of health-care users.

Another non-trivial detail: In order to get the figure of $3,000, Murray has instituted a $2,500 deductible. This essentially means that families without other resources will be able to see a doctor in a catastrophe but not for routine problems and prevention.

And then, of course, there is the issue of high-quality child care: a single parent who goes to work full-time is likely to spend his or her entire grant on child care. Even at three dollars an hour, care for one child will cost $120 per week, or about $500 per month, and if the parent has a low-wage job, his or her marginal tax rate becomes pretty steep even with one child, let alone two.

Dalton Conley, Boston Review,
September/October 2006.

consider ways of closing that gap through increased taxation or additional budget cuts, because the gap will disappear on its own in a few years."

There are several problems with this. First, even if everything else Murray says is true, financing that enormous gap for the next few years, with the public finances already deep in deficit, would be, well, challenging.

Second, this is to say nothing of the full transition costs of Murray's scheme, which the book makes no attempt to estimate. That gap of $355 billion, beginning in Year One, is not a transition cost; it's just the financial shortfall in a hypothetical equilibrium. Transition costs—which, at a guess, would be enormous—come on top of this, and would persist for decades.

Additional Costs

Consider Social Security. It might well be true that, fully phased in, Murray's scheme would allow all Americans to save enough to enjoy a higher income in retirement than they can expect to receive under the present system. But you cannot put today's actual and prospective Social Security recipients, who have not had 45 years to save for retirement under Murray's plan, on a flat annual income of $10,000 and expect to survive—not politically, and perhaps not literally. That is why, as with Social Security privatization (another good idea in principle), very large transition costs would persist for decades. This is not a minor detail, to be brushed away. It is a chief argument against.

Third, putting the instant shortfall and the ongoing transition costs aside, the cost paths that Murray is comparing are not very plausibly defined. Partly, that is because Murray is right that the costs of the present system are unsustainable. If the system is not dismantled, it will indeed be reformed, because it will have to be.

For instance, the retirement age will most likely be raised again, a seemingly small change that makes an enormous difference to Social Security's fiscal outlook. There will be many other patches and tweaks. Murray could fairly reply that extra years of work (or whatever) would then have to be counted as a cost of the existing system—but that is not the same as saying that the present system, once amended in this and other ways, as it surely must be, is structurally doomed.

At the same time, Murray probably underestimates the long-term cost of his universal $10,000 a year. He lets this grant rise in line with inflation, and he allows for further upward slippage (of about 1 percent a year) owing to demographic factors, but the annual payment stays constant in real terms. Fifty years from now—and Murray asks us to think that far ahead—views about what constitutes poverty will have changed, and an annual income of $10,000, even adjusted for inflation, is going to seem like a lot less than it does today.

And there will be other kinds of slippage. For his scheme to succeed, Murray understands the fiscal importance of replacing *all* welfare benefits with the $10,000 a year—hence his proposed constitutional amendment. But could this line be held, really? An income of $10,000 a year, together with a low-paid job held for just part of the year, is enough to lift an individual out of poverty (even allowing for saving and health costs).

Depending on Private Charity

But not everybody who does not work is idle or feckless: Many people, physically or mentally disabled, cannot work at all. In Murray's plan, private charity would be needed to keep them out of poverty. Never mind whether that would be a desirable state of affairs. (Murray thinks it would; I do not.) As a matter of sheer practicality, I find it politically unrealistic, actually hard to imagine, especially alongside a system that treats the able-bodied idle so well.

Murray asks readers to believe that his plan is not just affordable but fiscally compelling. As it stands, it is neither.

Fiscally speaking, its prospects are zero. . . . It would be far better for the country if the coming, unavoidable, piecemeal reform of the welfare state were guided, as far as possible, by some wise general principles. And Murray's arguments go directly to what those principles should be. He puts self-determination front and center. He wants to confront people with the consequences of their choices, to insist that people take responsibility for their own lives, and to give them the means to do so.

I think he is right to believe that the more this can be done, the better our societies will be.

Unfortunately, implementing this principle is a much harder thing than he allows—and his plan to do it all at one stroke cannot work.

Periodical Bibliography

The following articles have been selected to supplement the diverse views presented in this chapter.

American Prospect	"Ending Poverty in America," 16-Part Special Report, May 2007.
Jean Anyon and Kiersten Greene	"No Child Left Behind as an Anti-Poverty Measure," *Teacher Education Quarterly*, Spring 2007. www.publiceducation.org/pdf/ 2007_NCLB_Anti_Poverty.pdf.
Richard C. Cook	"Poverty in America: Progressive Schemes to Reduce Poverty Will Fail Without Monetary Reform," *Global Researcher*, June 7, 2007. www.globalresearch.ca/index.php?context =va&aid=5905.
Henry Fernandez	"Limited Benefits: Insurers Peddle 'Limited Health Care' to America's Working Poor," *Center for American Progress*, May 7, 2007.
Ron Haskins	"Fighting Poverty Through Incentives and Work Mandates for Young Men," Center on Children & Families, Brookings Institution, fall 2007. www.brookings.edu/papers/2007/fall_ poverty_haskins.aspx.
Howard Jacob Karger	"The 'Poverty Tax' and America's Low-Income Households" special issue: *Working but Poor, Families in Society*, July-September 2007.
Daniel Muniz	"Avoiding Poverty: Four Simple Rules to Follow," *National Summary*, December 2, 2007.
Stanford Center for the Study of Poverty and Inequality	"A New War on Poverty?" *Pathways*, Winter 2008.
Mark Winne	"The Futility of Food Banks: Generosity of Donors and Volunteers Hasn't Addressed Underlying Problem: Poverty," *Washington Post*, November 19, 2007.

CHAPTER 4

How Should Global
Poverty Be Addressed?

Chapter Preface

Microcredit may not yet be a household word, but it is certainly a buzzword in the debate over global poverty. The microcredit movement, and related financial services collectively called microfinance, has taken off across Asia, Africa, and Latin America. It is supported by wealthy foundations, nonprofit organizations, and financial institutions that are convinced of its potential to lift hundreds of millions of destitute people out of poverty and transform the developing world.

As journalist Patricia Yollin wrote simply in 2007, microcredit is "very small loans to very poor people for very small businesses." The idea's most successful advocate is Bangladeshi economist Muhammad Yunus, who realized in 1976 that loans of less than a hundred dollars could make a huge difference in the lives of poor, illiterate Bangladeshi women who lacked the collateral to get bank loans. Yunus founded the Grameen Bank exclusively to serve the poorest of the poor, who used their microcredit loans to buy sewing machines, a dairy cow, materials to make bamboo stools, and a range of other items that enabled them to earn a living.

Yunus proved that the poor could be reliable borrowers: Today Grameen boasts a loan recovery rate of 98.35 percent and finances 100 percent of its loans by borrower deposits alone. Yollin points to examples of microcredit in action on three continents: "A Peruvian widow borrowed $64 and bought a few pigs. For $55, a villager in Ghana went into the mineral-water trade. A mother of nine in Guatemala upgraded her grocery store with $250." According to *New Yorker* writer Connie Bruck, Yunus says microcredit gets results:

> More than fifty per cent of the Grameen Bank's borrowers who have been in the program for more than five years have risen out of poverty, according to a simple measurement

that he himself devised. (To have graduated from poverty, a family must have, among other things, a house with a tin roof; clean drinking water; a sanitary latrine; warm clothes for winter and mosquito netting for summer; about seventy-five dollars in a savings account; and schooling for the children.)

Microcredit has its detractors. First, there is sometimes bitter division within the movement over the commercialization that has followed its success. Yunus wants to keep the focus on microcredit to the poorest of the poor. He objects to microfinance entrepreneurs and investors who, in a drive for profitability, are more likely to selectively qualify only the "less poor" for loans. Second, some critics charge that microcredit is only a palliative measure, not much-needed societal reform, and that interest rates approaching 20 percent actually burden the poor with debt. Others say microcredit is not good if it absolves governments of the responsibility for addressing poverty. And some worry about the hyperbole surrounding microcredit, fearing support will dwindle when unrealistic expectations are not met. Nevertheless, endorsement and awareness of microcredit is growing, and likely to influence the ongoing debate over solutions to global poverty represented by the viewpoints in this chapter.

> *"The population share of the extreme poor in developing countries [is] projected to fall from 29 percent in 1990 to 12 percent by 2015."*

The UN Millennium Project Can Halve Global Poverty by 2015

The World Bank

In September 2000 the United Nations adopted eight core goals known as the Millennium Development Goals (MDGs) to fight global poverty, illiteracy, gender inequality, child mortality, HIV/ AIDS and other epidemics, and environmental degradation. In 2002 a broad partnership including the 189 UN member nations, international financial institutions such as the World Bank and International Monetary Fund, nongovernmental organizations, and private-sector researchers and scientists produced an action plan for achieving the MDGs with time-bound, measurable targets; for example, achieving MDG1, "Eradicate extreme poverty and hunger," means cutting in half the share of the world's population living on less than a dollar a day by 2015. In the following viewpoint, the World Bank, the world's primary anti-poverty lending and grant-distribution organization to developing countries, reports progress—the proportion of the world's extreme poor fell from 29 percent in 1990 to 18 percent in 2004, and is projected to fall to 12 percent by 2015.

As you read, consider the following questions:

1. Despite overall population growth in developing countries, by how much did the absolute number of extremely poor people fall between 1999 and 2004, in the World Bank's assessment?
2. According to the World Bank, which two regions will reduce extreme poverty by far more than half, and which region will fail to meet the MDG1 target?
3. What conditions define fragile states, and why is poverty reduction so difficult to achieve in these countries, according to the author?

Under the first Millennium Development Goal (MDG1), the international community aims to halve the global rate of extreme income poverty—as measured by the share of the population living on less than $1 per day—between 1990 and 2015. Current trends and growth forecasts indicate that this goal will be achieved, although not in Sub-Saharan Africa. High growth in China and India explains much of the reduction in the global poverty rate, although progress toward MDG1 has also quickened in many other developing countries. High growth has continued in most of the developing world in [2006–2007] as a result of better policies in developing countries and a favorable global environment. The outlook for growth and poverty reduction remains favorable, although some risks remain. In particular, low-income country per capita growth is expected to remain above 5 percent in 2007.

Keys to Development

Addressing the problems of fragile states is central to the development agenda and to furthering progress toward the MDGs? ["Fragile states" refers to countries that face particularly severe challenges, such as deteriorating government, prolonged crisis or violence, or a legacy of conflict.] Nine percent of the population, and about 27 percent of the extreme poor in developing countries live in fragile states. This situation will not improve unless fragile states become less vulnerable to adverse shocks, and they increase their capacity to absorb external funds and to mobilize internal resources for sustained poverty reduction and improved economic security....

[This viewpoint] reports on recent progress in further areas covered in last year's *Global Monitoring Report* (GMR) 2006 that are central to achieving higher sustained growth, promotion of a better investment climate, and improvements in governance. A better investment climate is key to attaining higher growth and employment creation, while, as noted in [2006's] GMR, governance is an ongoing part of MDG monitoring, because it is an important factor underpinning a country's development effectiveness and progress toward the MDGs.

While higher economic growth is generally desirable, one should also be aware of its environmental costs. Although the recent boom in commodity prices has helped to underpin strong growth in many of the most natural resource–dependent economies, high resource dependence can lead to high rates of resource depletion. Countries are liquidating assets when they extract minerals and energy, harvest forests and fish unsustainably, or deplete their agricultural soils, and this can have consequences for future growth.

Gender equality—in the sense of equality of opportunities, not outcomes—plays an important role in development. Cross-country data show an inverse relationship between the incidence of poverty and the level of gender equality as measured by the rate of female labor market participation. Greater gender equality in access to education, land, technology, and credit markets is also associated with lower poverty. While the direction of causality of these relationships is unclear, it is evident that higher gender equality is associated with better MDG outcomes, including higher nutritional status and lower poverty.

Progress on Poverty Reduction

The prospects for achieving MDG1—halving poverty by 2015—are largely unchanged from [the 2006] *Global Monitoring Report*. Overall, the world as a whole is on track to meet the goal with the population share of the extreme poor in developing countries projected to fall from 29 percent in 1990 to 12 percent in 2015. By 2004, over halfway through the goal period, this share had already dropped to 18 percent. Preliminary estimates suggest that the number of extremely poor people in developing countries fell by 135 million between 1999 and 2004.

This positive assessment overshadows significant regional differences. Sub-Saharan Africa remains a long way off the path that would take it to MDG1, even assuming projected growth rates higher than the historic averages since 1990. Between 1999 and 2004, the share of people in extreme poverty in the region fell to 41 percent, a decline of 4.7 percentage points, but higher population growth left the same absolute number of poor at nearly 300 million. The region now accounts for 30 percent of the world's extreme poor, compared with 19 percent in 1990 and only 11 percent in 1981. The Europe and Central Asia region has lost ground since 1990, and may not meet the development goal. The Middle East and North Africa region is expected to achieve MDG1, albeit narrowly, while the Latin America and Caribbean region is likely to come close. However, the main drivers of poverty reduction globally continue to be countries in the East Asia and Pacific

[EAP] and South Asia [SA] regions, which—thanks to spectacular rates of growth in the last decade—are both set to overshoot the poverty target. By 2015, extreme poverty rates are projected to be below 3 percent for EAP countries, and 18 percent for SA countries, as compared to MDG1 targets of 15 and 22 percent respectively.

For a number of countries, it is possible to go beyond the regional estimates and use poverty estimates from household surveys to examine whether, for a typical country, the upturn in growth since the late 1990s led to poverty reduction. The countries included are those with household surveys conducted during both the middle/late 1990s and after 2001. The results must be interpreted with caution in view of possible survey measurement and sampling errors, and, in view of the limited number of countries for which there are appropriate data, may not be representative of entire regions or country groups. Furthermore, the relationship between growth and poverty may be obscured by changes in relative prices, taxes and transfers, including worker remittances, and, as noted below, changes in income distribution.

In low-income countries the preliminary estimates suggest that, on average, growth has clearly resulted in lower poverty incidence: for a sample of 19 low-income countries, 1 percent of GDP [gross domestic product] growth was associated with a 1.3 percent fall in the rate of extreme poverty and a 0.9 percent fall in the $2-a-day poverty rate. Clear poverty impacts are also evident in the three regions for which sufficient country-level data are available. The picture is somewhat different for middle-income countries where the impact of GDP per capita growth on poverty was less. While a high negative elasticity was obtained for the Latin America and the Caribbean sample by the $2-a-day poverty definition, this reflects increased poverty in a context of near-zero negative growth. One hypothesis is that the poor in the middle-income countries examined were drawn relatively heavily from economically productive groups, who did not enjoy the benefits of growth given its sectoral and geographic composition, and from groups such as retirees and the unemployed, who may depend substantially on public transfers.

There was also a somewhat different impact of growth on poverty incidence in China and India. In China, high growth led to very substantial decreases in poverty rates, while in India, the gains in poverty reduction were more modest. In both countries, poverty reduction took place despite a worsening of the income distribution. Between 1981 and 2004, there was an estimated decline in the absolute number of extreme poor in China of over 500 million people, while in India, the number of extreme poor remained roughly constant.

Changes in income distribution have not, on average, reduced the impact of income growth on poverty reduction in low-income countries. Inequality in income as measured by the Gini index [a statistical tool for measuring income inequality] declined on average for the overall sample of low-income countries. In contrast, income inequality widened on average in middle-income countries, thus hindering poverty reduction.

Improvements in Long-Term Growth

It is reassuring that the pick-up in low-income-country per capita growth rates that started in the 1990s continued in 2006 with an estimated overall per capita GDP growth of 5.9 percent, up from an average of 4.0 percent in 2001–05. As in previous years, most regions show strong growth performance, with a particularly impressive rate of growth in the low-income countries of Europe and Central Asia, which are still experiencing a rebound after the transition recession of the mid-1990s. The region continues to benefit from strong commodity prices and export earnings. In South Asia, growth in India continues at a formidable pace, but other countries in the region are also doing well with the exception of Nepal,

---

The Multilateral Debt Relief Initiative (MDRI)

(Per-capita income at or below US$380)	(Per-capita income at or above US$380)
25 Countries that have benefited from MDRI [100 percent debt cancellation] as of end-December, 2007	
Burkina Faso, Cambodia, Ethiopia, The Gambia, Ghana, Madagascar, Malawi, Mali, Mozambique, Niger, Rwanda, São Tomé and Principe, Sierra Leone, Tajikistan, Tanzania, Uganda	Benin, Bolivia, Cameroon, Guyana, Honduras, Mauritania, Nicaragua, Senegal, Zambia
18 Countries that will be eligible once they reach the completion point under the Enhanced HIPC Initiative	
Afghanistan, Burundi, Central African Republic, Chad, Democratic Republic of the Congo, Guinea-Bssau, Eritrea, Liberia, Nepal, Togo	Guinea, Haiti, Republic of Congo, Comoros, Côte d'Ivoire, Kyrgyz Republic, Sudan

Precise data on the per capita income of Somalia are not available at this juncture.

TAKEN FROM: International Monetary Fund, "The Multilateral Debt Relief Initiative (MDRI)," December 2007.

---

which has been suffering from political unrest. Most importantly, in view of the high poverty in the region, Sub-Saharan African countries are also experiencing sustained and rising growth rates. Oil-exporting countries have contributed significantly to this strong performance. Increased oil production and the large terms-of-trade gains from the oil price hike have boosted domestic incomes and spending. Non-fuel-exporting African countries seem to have weathered the adverse shock of high oil prices well, thanks to a mixture of improved policies and strong non-fuel commodity prices. In contrast with the high rates of per capita growth in other regions, growth among low-income countries in the Middle East and North Africa and Latin America and the Caribbean regions continues to be much lower.

Growth in middle-income countries also continues to be strong. China remains the star performer with an estimated per capita growth of 10 percent in 2006. But other middle-income countries in the region and elsewhere are also growing at sustained rates, thus improving prospects for the gradual reduction of the pockets of poverty that still exist in these countries. Recent outcomes suggest that per capita growth rates in middle-income countries have increased, with average rates in the last few years significantly and consistently higher than pre-2000 values.

Weak Growth in Fragile States

Fragile states have consistently grown more slowly than other low-income countries. Although the average per capita growth of such states has picked up in recent years, this is partly due to accelerated expansion in a few fuel-producing countries and a fall in the number of conflicts. Among non-fuel-producing fragile states, while growth has increased since 2000, the outlook is for per capita growth to remain a full percentage point lower than that experienced by low-income countries as a whole. Lower investment relative to GDP in fragile states linked in part to lower national savings rates (domestic savings and net transfers from abroad, including official transfers and worker remittances) has been one cause of their slower growth.

Clearly the inferior growth performance of fragile states has been, and is likely to continue to be, an obstacle to the achievement of MDG1. Fragile states are home to 9 percent of the population of developing countries, and have nearly twice the incidence of extreme poverty of other low-income countries. About 27 percent of the extreme poor in developing countries live in fragile states. Moreover, fragile states can have adverse spillovers on neighboring countries through conflict, refugee flows, organized crime, spread of epidemic diseases, and barriers to trade and investment.

The rate of extreme poverty in the current set of fragile states is estimated to have risen somewhat in 1990–2004 from 49 percent to over 54 percent. The projected poverty rate for this group of countries in 2015 is slightly higher than in 1990 under current assumptions about future growth and income distribution, suggesting that no overall progress will be made toward MDG1 over the goal period as a whole. In contrast, nonfragile states made significant progress in reducing poverty by 2004, and are projected to overachieve MDG1 by 2015.

Conflicts have undermined growth performance at various times in most fragile states. Conflicts are a major reason why countries slide into fragility; they extract high costs in terms of lives and physical damage, but also reduce growth and increase poverty. There is consensus in the relevant literature that civil conflict reduces GDP growth, although estimates of the size of this impact vary. The impact of conflict on growth and poverty incidence seems to have worsened since the beginning of the 1990s. Conflicts have become shorter and more intense than before; their average impact on GDP growth is now about −12 percent per year of conflict. While in the past, the fall in growth was more gradual, and was followed by a gradual and prolonged recovery within the conflict period, since 1990 the period of the growth collapse has largely coincided with that of the conflict, leading to this higher annual GDP loss. It has also taken longer for countries to regain their preconflict per capita income levels than would have been the case before 1990.

Because conflict is both a major cause and consequence of poverty in fragile states, the coherence and sequencing of international diplomatic, security, and development engagement is more important in these environments than elsewhere. Recent research demonstrates that the risk of reversion to conflict is significantly higher in the period following postconflict elections than in the period preceding elections. This increased risk does not diminish for the first postconflict decade. In discussions of these results at the United Nations (UN) Peace-Building Commission, participants noted that this risk may have important implications for the sequencing of electoral, peacekeeping, and development assistance, underlining the importance of efforts to ensure that electoral assistance in fragile transitions is properly sequenced with decisions to maintain or draw down peace-keeping troops, and with aid-financed efforts to support measures to generate growth and employment and other initiatives that may mitigate the risks of reversion to conflict.

Why Fragile States Stay Fragile

Conflict aside, all fragile states have weak institutions and governance, hindering growth. Some states may be willing to promote growth and reduce poverty, but are unable to do so for a variety of reasons such as a lack of territorial control, political cohesion, and administrative capacity. In other states, governments may be unwilling to take necessary actions because they are not substantively committed to overall poverty reduction, or they may promote poverty reduction while excluding certain social or geographical groups.

State fragility has proven to be a persistent condition. Of the 34 states judged as fragile in 1980, 21 were still viewed as such in 2005, although of these, 6 had left and later resumed fragile status during the period. The average duration of fragility among the 2005 group of fragile states was 16.6 years. For the 20 countries that entered and permanently left the fragile states list since 1980, the average duration of fragility was 7.8 years. Of these, Mozambique experienced the shortest duration of fragility (3 years), and Niger the longest (15 years).

Nevertheless there are some success stories. Specifically, Vietnam, Mozambique, and Uganda have graduated from fragile state status. All three experienced severe violent conflict but managed to achieve a durable cessation of hostilities. Conflict ended either because there was a change in geopolitical conditions that provided incentives for warring parties to lay down their arms, or because there was a military victory by one party involved in the conflict that eliminated opposition groups or gave them a stake in the postconflict political order. Subsequently in all three countries, growth was enabled by the introduction of at least modest programs of market-oriented economic reform that were managed so as to keep interested elites on board.

Limited capacity and willingness to undertake needed reforms in fragile states undermine the mainstream poverty reduction approach based on partnership as exemplified by the

Poverty Reduction Strategy Paper (PRSP). Difficulties donors experience when working in these countries, particularly the ones with limited geopolitical relevance, can lead to excessively low or volatile aid flows even after taking into account the countries' low level of governance. The international community is increasingly aware of issues particular to fragile states, and has been considering alternative approaches tailored to the characteristics of specific countries, for example, emphasizing humanitarian assistance and relying where possible on help from nonstate actors such as nongovernmental organizations (NGOs).

"*Six years into this war on poverty the [Millennium Development] goals are mired in a devil's brew of self-serving economic policies, lethargic bureaucracy, and outright disingenuousness.*"

The UN Millennium Project Is Failing to Reduce Global Poverty

Conn Hallinan

Conn Hallinan is a foreign policy analyst for the think tank Foreign Policy in Focus, a joint project of Washington, DC's International Relations Center and the Institute for Policy Studies. He is also a journalism lecturer at the University of California, Santa Cruz. In this viewpoint, Hallinan challenges World Bank and International Monetary Fund claims that the UN Millennium Project can cut global poverty in half by 2015. On the contrary, Hallinan argues, hunger and privation levels have hardly changed over the past decade and in some cases are even worse—he cites India in particular, a country touted by the Millennium Project as leading the way in poverty reduction.

Conn Hallinan, "The Devil's Brew of Poverty Relief," *Foreign Policy in Focus Commentary*, July 19, 2006, pp. 1–4. Copyright © 2006 IRC and IPS. www.fpic.org. All rights reserved. Reproduced by permission.

As you read, consider the following questions:

1. According to Hallinan, debt relief to poor countries is the only aid initiative on schedule. Why has debt relief failed to reduce poverty even though this aspect of Millenniun Goal 1 is on track, in Hallinan's view?

2. How does U.S. agricultural policy prevent economic growth in the poorest of the least developed countries, in the author's view?

3. How should the delivery of international food aid be reformed to help the poor, according to the author?

O nce a year or so, the topic of poverty climbs onto the agenda for the developed world. Poverty was a theme at [the 2005] Group of 8 (G8) meeting, and [in 2007] when the United States, Canada, Japan, Britain, Russia, Germany, France, and Italy [sat] down in Berlin to divvy up the global economy. But [in 2006] in St. Petersburg, energy policy (and the Middle East) dominated the G8 discussions, and the topic of poverty barely surfaced.

The venues shift, the faces at the table change, but the hard facts about hunger and privation are not much different than they were a decade ago. In some cases the situation has gotten worse.

- Over 90% of urban populations have no access to safe drinking water and, by [2007] more than half of the world will live in cities. The slums of Mumbai [formerly called Bombay, India] have more people than the entire country of Norway.

- One third of the world's population—2.3 billion people—have no access to toilets or latrines, a major reason for the 13 million annual deaths ascribed to water-borne diseases.

- Almost 47% of children in Bangladesh and India are malnourished. Life expectancy in most of Africa is less than 50 years, and in those countries ravaged by AIDS, less than 40 years.

- Hunger and malnutrition is worse in sub-Saharan Africa than it was a decade ago.

Back in 2000, the United Nations established a Millennium Development Goal to halve global poverty by 2015. The G8's enormous wealth, along with its dominance in world trade, was to play the key role in this worldwide assault on poverty and disease.

But six years into this war on poverty the goals are mired in a devil's brew of self-serving economic policies, lethargic bureaucracy, and outright disingenuousness. Only South America and the Caribbean are even approaching the Millennium targets.

The Downside of Debt Relief

Meeting in 2005 in Gleneagles, Scotland, the G8 pledged to prioritize Africa for debt relief, accelerated aid, and increased trade. A year later, most of those initiatives are bogged down. The only part of the program running on schedule is debt relief, which looks good on paper but translates into very little on the ground. Indeed, debt forgiveness ends up benefiting the donors much of the time.

For instance, the World Bank, the International Monetary Fund, and the African Development bank cancelled more than $40 billion in debts to nineteen countries. But according to the *Financial Times*, while the "face value" of the debt was $40 billion, "it cost rich countries just $1.2 billion a year to write off."

Most of the G8 increase in aid—from $80 billion in 2004 to $106.5 billion in 2005—was in debt write offs. Very little of that money went toward upgrading water systems, improving disease control, or increasing food consumption.

If debt reduction is removed from the aid packages, German aid fell 8%, and France and Britain's dipped 2%. And while U.S. foreign aid jumped 16%, if you subtract Iraq and Afghanistan, it actually declined 4%.

Debt relief is important and allows developing countries to divert interest payments toward upgrading their infrastructures. But it is also a cheap way for developed countries to fulfill their aid obligations.

When it comes to the White House and aid, what you see is not necessarily what you get. For instance, according to David Bryden of the Global AIDS Alliance, the [George W.] Bush administration's 2005 pledge to "double" aid to Africa translated into only 9% in new spending, and much of that will not appear until after 2008. The rest was funding to which the Congress and the administration were already committed.

Even when aid is promised, it may never appear. In the 2002 Monterrey Consensus—named after the city in Mexico where the conference took place—the G8 pledged that each member would deliver 0.7% of its gross national product in aid. But before the ink was dry, the Bush administration argued that the pledge was simply a "guideline," even though paragraph 42 of the Consensus binds the signers to the formula.

And if aid does materialize, it may not arrive on time. A recent study by the British-based charity, Save the Children, found that the European Commission—the world's second largest aid donor—along with key members of the G8, were consistently tardy in dispersing their assistance packages. The report blamed the delays on bureaucracy and inefficient administration.

"Delays in disbursing budget support can mean that teachers and health workers don't get paid, or that important medical supplies and school textbooks don't reach the children who need them," Sarah Hague, Save the Children's economic adviser, told the *Financial Times*.

The Problem in Washington

A major roadblock to improving the lives of billions of people is the refusal of the United States to consider opening its agricultural markets, even as it insists that developing countries open theirs. This is particularly important in Africa, where 50% of a country's GNP [gross national product] may be in agriculture.

The U.S. government heavily subsidizes crops like corn, soy, cotton, and wheat, so that U.S. wheat sells for 46% below production cost, with corn at 20% below cost. If Brazil or South Korea were to try to do the same thing with steel, they would be accused of "dumping" on the international market.

The G8 members of the European Union (EU) argue that if developing countries remove their tariffs, they will be overwhelmed with cheap U.S. produce, which will drive their farmers out of business, encourage uneven regional development, and do very little to aid the poor.

Mexico and the North American Free Trade Agreement (NAFTA) is a case in point. Mexican fruit and vegetable exports increased 50% under NAFTA, enriching big landowners in the country's north. But U.S.-subsidized corn is swamping small farmers in the south. Some two million farmers have left the land, and 18 million subsist on less than two dollars a day, accelerating rural poverty and helping to fuel the growth of immigration.

Mexican wheat production has fallen 50%, and U.S. imports now account for 99% of Mexico's soybeans, 80% of its rice, 30% of its chicken, beef, and pork, and 33% of its beans. When Mexican cattle growers switched from sorghum to cheaper U.S. corn, they put the local sorghum industry out of business.

While the United States demands the removal of foreign barriers, it maintains tariffs on sugar and cotton, two crops that are, coincidentally, central to the key electoral battleground states of Florida and Texas.

Developing World Becoming a Giant Slum

[Mike Davis:] Over a billion people live in slums world-wide, and the number of actually poor people living in cities is greater than that. So, not quite a sixth of the world's 6.5 billion inhabitants. But that [slum] population will double by 2020, and the build-out of the human race will achieve its maximum sometime just after the middle of the century: 10 billion people. At that point slum dwellers will be 20 percent of the total.

Almost all of the increase [in slum residents] was occurring in cities of the Third World. The rural world has reached its maximum population, and even declined. All the additional humans born on this planet will be born in cities. A large proportion of them, unfortunately, will be housed in slums. . . .

For the last 25 or 30 years, the World Bank and international organizations have written off the ability of states, of governments in the Third World, to provide either housing or jobs for the poor. What they've counted on is self-built housing, [achieved] basically through squatting on the periphery of cities. And secondly, through the so-called informal sector, where people essentially create their own jobs in one form or another.

Mike Davis, interviewed by Juris Jurjevics,
San Diego Reader, April 3, 2006.

According to the *Financial Times*, "new research suggests that the very poorest of the least developed countries (LDCs) could make big gains in exports and growth if the United States followed the EU and opened its markets to LDC."

Free trade has been a disaster for most the developing world. In Latin America, where until recently the free trade

"Washington Consensus" held sway, growth from 1987 to 2002 averaged 1.5%. To put a dent in poverty, Latin America requires a growth rate of at least 4% or more.

The EU is also part of the problem. While it has been critical of U.S. intransigence on tariffs, the EU has kept out a number of LDC exports over health issues, and it subsidizes its farmers as well. In all, the developed world hands out nearly $1 billion in farm subsidies each day.

Reforming Food Aid

Food aid policy in the United States, for which the total 2005 budget was $1.6 billion, is largely dictated by an "iron triangle" of agribusiness, shipping magnates, and charity foundations. Studies demonstrate that the most efficient way to deliver aid is to purchase food locally rather than buy and ship it from the donor country.

But Washington insists that food aid must come from the United States, be shipped on U.S. carriers, and distributed by agencies like CARE and Catholic Relief Services. As a result, 60 cents out of every aid dollar goes to middlemen for transport, storage, and distribution.

Four companies and their subsidiaries, led by agri-giants Archer Daniels Midland and Cargill, sell more than half the food used by the Agency for International Development. Five big shipping companies dominate the transport side of the equation. And relief agencies, like CARE and Catholic Relief Services, generate up to half their budgets by selling some of the aid food.

Oxfam has long lobbied for putting cash directly into the hands of local farmers rather than handing it out to agricultural and transport corporations, but most U.S. aid groups support the current system and so has the U.S. Congress. CARE, however, recently broke ranks and endorsed the Oxfam initiative.

The recent G8 meeting largely tabled the issue for [2006], but the problem is not going to go away. Poverty is an affliction of the underdeveloped world, but the solutions to it lie in altering the policies of the developed world.

> "[Multinational corporations] are the only institutions that have the resources and competence required to reduce poverty sustainably."

Multinational Corporations Can Reduce Global Poverty

George C. Lodge and Craig Wilson

George C. Lodge, assistant secretary of labor for international affairs under Presidents Dwight D. Eisenhower and John F. Kennedy, is the Jaime and Josefina Chua Tiampo Professor of Business Administration Emeritus at Harvard Business School, and coauthor of A Corporate Solution to Global Poverty *with Craig Wilson, an economist with the International Finance Corporation based in Bangladesh. In the following viewpoint, Lodge and Wilson defend and promote the role of multinational corporations (MNCs) in the developing world. Reducing poverty anywhere, they argue, depends on business growth, and big business knows best how to give small local businesses access to markets, credit, and technology. Moreover, globalization means big business is providing jobs, infrastructure, and educational opportunity to the poorest of the poor, more than their own governments can offer.*

George C. Lodge and Craig Wilson, "Multinational Corporations: A Key to Global Poverty Reduction," *YaleGlobal Online*, January 2, 2006. Copyright © 2006 Yale Center for the Study of Globalization. Reproduced by permission.

As you read, consider the following questions:

1. How did MNC programs help subsistence farmers in Panama emerge from poverty, according to Lodge and Wilson?

2. How have Nestlé and DaimlerChrysler projects reduced poverty and proved that sustainable change requires profit-seeking ventures, according to the authors?

3. Why do Lodge and Wilson propose the establishment of the World Development Corporation?

The world's multinational corporations (MNCs)—63,000 of them at last count—frequently find themselves the target of criticism by the world's anti-globalization protesters. MNCs, the protesters charge, are principally responsible for the impoverishment of many of the world's six billion people.

While global corporations have unquestionably brought greater wealth, power and opportunity to the poor world, especially China and India, according to the World Bank some two billion people still live in countries or regions that have been left behind, becoming in fact less globalized. In these places trade has diminished in relation to national income, foreign investment and economic growth have stagnated, and poverty has risen. Most Africans were better off 40 years ago. The average per capita income of Muslims—from Morocco to Bangladesh and beyond to Indonesia and the Philippines—is half the world average. Thus while globalization has benefited many, one-sixth of the world's people live in what the International Finance Corporation [IFC] calls "deep poverty," as described in a 2004 speech by Peter Woicke, then IFC's executive vice president.

The causes of poverty are many and varied. Rightly or wrongly, many blame the corporations that drive globalization. Belligerence is escalating. For example, at a recent meeting of the World Economic Forum anti-globalization protesters waved signs reading: "Our resistance is as global as your oppression."

Poverty Reduction Depends on MNCs

This decline in corporate legitimacy, coupled with governance failures, need not prevent actions by MNCs to reduce global poverty. Indeed, we argue that such challenges make those activities all the more critical. Without harnessing the support of the world's great MNCs, the UN's Millenium Development Goal to halve the number of people living on less than $1 a day by 2015 will be difficult to attain.

MNC involvement is crucial to poverty reduction for two reasons: First, the reduction of poverty depends on the growth of business, especially small, domestic businesses. And increasingly for a local business to flourish it must have access to the world: to markets, credit, and technology, all facilitated by MNCs. The second reason is less obvious and more controversial: Poverty reduction requires systemic change, and MNCs are the world's most efficient and sustainable engines of change. They provide political leverage with local governments; they offer opportunity for people who are convinced there is none; they motivate the young to learn and organize to gain power; they build roads and hospitals and other infrastructure. MNCs in developing countries are often the first choice for private-sector jobs by young people, who are attracted by the higher salaries and the learning opportunities. And wise governments get the private sector to do as much spending on infrastructure as possible in order to protect their own treasuries.

Many of the world's poor live in countries where governments lack either the desire or the ability to raise living standards on their own. Financial assistance to such countries— some $2.5 trillion has been provided in the last 50 years—has often not helped neediest citizens. In fact, it may have worsened their plight by sustaining the corrupt or otherwise inefficient governments that contribute to their misery, by leaving nations with mountainous debt.

Examples of MNCs in Action

In such mismanaged countries—as many as 70 around the world—a way must be found to change the basic system. Many multinationals have done just this, as a matter of course, while at the same time making the profits upon which their survival depends. Nestlé and Unilever in India, Coca-Cola in Venezuela, Intel in Costa Rica, and Land O' Lakes International in Albania are but a few examples. Their initiatives not only provide jobs and raise incomes; they also improve education and give individuals motivation to pursue it. Education, after all, requires more than just buildings, teachers and texts. In much of the developing world, the poor lack faith that change is possible; few believe in the existence of a social or economic ladder that, with proper education, they can use to climb out of poverty.

A number of years ago, one of the authors and his students worked in Veraguas Province, Panama, to help a progressive bishop, Marcos McGrath, establish credit and marketing cooperatives to raise the incomes of desperately poor subsistence farmers. Only after the people realized that change was possible did they see the value of education. They created their own school, and engaged a teacher who taught children how to fix refrigerators acquired from the Canal Zone. Education had begun. The bishop's cooperative movement was an engine of change. It was resisted by the status quo. A priest was killed, but nevertheless the movement survived and today runs the biggest chicken factory in Central America.

In the province next to Veraguas, Nestlé followed much the same procedures as the bishop and his young organizers, agitating, motivating and organizing farmers for milk production. The difference was that Nestlé made a profit. Church money, charity or tax revenue alone cannot bring about the change required to reduce global poverty. Sustainable change requires profit-seeking ventures.

The success of a DaimlerChrysler project in Brazil's poverty-stricken northeast provides another example of a corporation changing the system to reduce poverty. In 1992, under pressure from the Green Party in Germany, DaimlerBenz, as it was then known, looked for ways to use renewable natural fibers in its automobiles. At the same time, the Brazilian government demanded that manufacturing facilities in the country increase their local content. To address both problems, the head of Daimler in Brazil arranged with POEMA, a local anti-poverty program in Belem, to construct a modern, high-tech factory that would make headrests and seats out of coco fibers from locally grown trees. As of today some 5,200 people are employed in this project. For these formerly impoverished Brazilians, life dramatically changed for the better: Children attend school, people are active in local politics, and health facilities have improved.

MNCs have the unmatched power and competence to reduce global poverty. Increasingly, world opinion, as well as the inclinations of their own managers and staff, urges MNCs to use that power more effectively. But MNCs lack a vehicle to make that transition in a sustainable and legitimate way. . . .

Barriers to Collaboration

Multinational corporations reduce poverty by connecting local business with world markets and bringing access to credit and technology. As efficient engines of change, MNCs also alter the conditions that create poverty. Yet MNCs are absent from some of the poorest regions in the world. The risks of investment are too high. So, the potential benefits of MNCs are not reaching the world's neediest places. There is a gap between need and investment. The challenge is to close that gap: to facilitate investment by MNCs in poor regions by minimizing risk, and by making the investment profitable and thus sustainable. To address this challenge, we propose a new institution, the World Development Corporation (WDC).

Reducing global poverty has become a top priority for world leaders in recent years, and a plethora of international agencies aim to help the poor: civil society organizations or NGOs [nongovernmental organizations], the United Nations and its specialized agencies, the World Bank and others. Yet overall, the efforts to reduce poverty have been disappointing.

Leaders of NGOs and development institutions have begun to realize that there is no way that they can sustainably reduce global poverty without the active involvement of MNCs. In the past, attempts at collaboration encountered strong resistance. That resistance, while diminishing, lingers today and rests on two pillars, one ideological and one structural.

The ideological problem is exemplified by the efforts of the UN Development Programme (UNDP) to collaborate with big business. In July 1998, eleven MNCs had agreed to participate in planning for a Global Sustainable Development Facility. The fierce opposition of NGOs, however, forced the UNDP to abort the project later that same year. The NGOs feared that the companies would "contaminate" the UNDP.

Another disconnect between the business of development and the world's MNCs is the absence of any meaningful participation by the MNCs in the preparation of World Bank/ International Monetary Fund Poverty Reduction Strategy Papers. These papers, which have had a most positive effect on development work, are drafted with and by client governments. But curiously the major companies that will actually drive poverty reduction are not at the table. Presumably the supposition is that government and business are and should be entirely separate, and that business is not a central ingredient in the poverty-reducing recipe.

The structural problem is that there is no institution with the capability and responsibility to design a coherent business-led approach to poverty reduction in a particular country and to connect it to the essential players: required MNCs, interested NGOs, local business partners, the local government, and multinational development agencies such as the World Bank and the UN.

Growing Sustainable Business

Some progress has been made to resolve these problems. The UNDP, acting under a new initiative called Growing Sustainable Business, works with Shell [Oil Company] and other companies to establish solar-powered irrigation systems in Ethiopia, and with Ericsson, ABB and other companies to bring electrification and telecommunications to Tanzania. NGOs, together with local business and government, are partners in these projects.

A particularly promising venture is the Investment Climate Facility for Africa, launched in November 2005 by a group of companies and development partners including Royal Dutch Shell, Anglo American, and the UK's Department for International Development. Working closely with a number of other local companies, NGOs and African governments, this facility, which is still under development, is to be owned and directed by the private sector. Its goal is to increase business investment in Africa through policy improvements in the investment climate.

While this work in the policy field is crucial, much more needs to be done to harness the capabilities of global corporations to reduce poverty. A WDC is necessary. The commercially oriented investment-making corporation could be established under the auspices of the UN, owned and managed by a Board composed of 12 or so MNCs which have had long and respected experience in developing countries, companies like Nestlé, Unilever, Shell, BP, Ericsson, ABB, Tata Industries, and Cemex. These companies would be called the partners and become the WDC shareholders. They would provide the initial funding, although funds could also come from OECD [Organization for Economic Cooperation and Development]

Reducing Poverty with Microloans

Imagine you are a poor woman in Bangladesh. You work hard almost every day weaving mats. In five days you can finish a mat that sells for less than a dollar. When your children get sick, there is no money for medicine. How much would it change your life, if you could borrow $65 to buy a sewing machine?

The above example is real. Joygon Begum was a poor mat weaver in Bangladesh. Joygon used her $65 loan from the Grameen Bank to buy a second-hand sewing machine, and started a small business making clothes, which her husband sells in the village market. Before her first loan, Joygon and her family frequently went hungry, and never had money for family medical care. She could not afford even the very small education fees for her children. Now, the family eats three healthy meals a day, with a diet including vegetables, grains, and a small amount of meat and fish. Her children attend school, and she has money saved up for emergencies. Small examples such as this are a reflection of an emerging international industry.

In the last 20 years, the "microfinance industry" has emerged. During the 1980's and 1990's, particularly in Asia, Africa, and Latin America, thousands of microfinance NGOs (Non-Government Organisations) were established to provide microloans, using individual and group lending methodologies. In the 1990's, while many of the NGOs failed to reach scale or financial sustainability, others led the way in demonstrating that:

—Poor people, particularly poor women, are excellent borrowers, when provided with efficient, responsive loan services at commercial rates.

Guy Vincent, Global Development Research Center, May 2005.

governments and development agencies. Representatives of the UN Secretary-General and the NGO community would also be on the board. An advisory committee drawn from developing countries, civil society organizations, businesses, academe, and development agencies would complement the board. The board would appoint a small staff composed of experts in development representing a broad range of countries.

The WDC would proceed experimentally, focusing on those countries or regions that have received little or no investment, those that have been left behind by the processes of globalization. In consultation with local governmental, business and community leaders, the WDC would identify and design project possibilities for the consideration of the WDC partners and affiliates who may join with them. After project selection, WDC staff would assist in finding local partners, and coordinate relations among the participating companies as well as with development agencies. Projects must be commercially sustainable and eventually profitable for the participating companies. In this way the WDC could close the gap between the intentions of international development agencies and the impoverished who wait for help.

Benefits for All

The WDC would encourage companies to work together and attack poverty on a broad front, bringing to bear their capabilities and resources. Nestlé, for example, might be accompanied in its dairy operations by companies providing electrification, telecommunications and micro-credit. Likewise, it would be rewarding for both the poor and the company if Globeleq, a subsidiary of the UK's Commonwealth Development Corporation that builds electric generating plants in developing countries, were to partner with companies that handle the distribution and uses of electricity. The WDC would shape and manage these kinds of partnerships.

The WDC would also coordinate assistance from local and foreign development partners to assist with projects. Likewise it would call on the services of NGOs, who after all are becoming the conscience of the world, to ensure that the project was fulfilling its objective of poverty reduction. And the WDC would also make use of UN resources whose stamp of approval would provide legitimacy.

We believe that MNC executives will welcome the WDC. It would provide an efficient way for them to do what they say they want to do at countless meetings and conferences: serve community needs, not as philanthropy but as a central component of their corporate strategy. In doing so, they will invigorate corporate legitimacy.

The WDC would facilitate critical partnerships between and among corporations, NGOs, governments and international agencies in a way that enhances the effectiveness of all partners. It would help open new markets for corporate goods and services, and offer corporate employees a means to personal fulfillment by involving them in contributing to the welfare of millions. Finally, it would contribute to the social and political stability of developing countries, which is beneficial to investors. In short, WDC projects would serve the interests not only of the poor but also—in the long run—of corporate shareholders.

MNCs have been the lightning rod of anti-globalization critics—sometimes with justification. At the same time, they are the only institutions that have the resources and competence required to reduce poverty sustainably in those countries that globalization has left behind. But they cannot succeed alone. Not only must they cooperate with one another, but they also must collaborate with other development agencies and organizations so that their efforts can legitimately benefit from public and governmental support.

> *"Loans, investments, and most forms of aid are designed not to fight poverty but to augment the wealth of transnational investors at the expense of local populations."*

Multinational Corporations Cause Global Poverty

Michael Parenti

Progressive political analyst and lecturer Michael Parenti sees little benefit to the millions living in extreme poverty, and considerable self-interest in multinational corporations' activities in the developing world. Far from fostering self-sufficiency, he argues in the following viewpoint, the transnationals buy up the best land for cash-crop exports, degrade the environment, and leave people already at subsistence level little choice but to move to overcrowded shantytowns where there are too few jobs to go around. Outsourcing boosts nothing but corporate profit margins, Parenti claims, and the already corrupt collaboration of government and big business should be discouraged as a poverty-reduction strategy. Michael Parenti is the author of Democracy for the Few *and a collection of essays,* Contrary Notions.

Michael Parenti, "Mystery: How Wealth Creates Poverty in the World," *Z Magazine*, April 26, 2007. Reproduced by permission of the author.

As you read, consider the following questions:

1. What does Parenti cite as the three main attractions of poor regions of Asia, Africa, and Latin America to transnational corporations?

2. How do corporations exploit the poor in Haiti, in the author's example?

3. How do structural adjustment programs (SAPs) imposed by the World Bank and International Monetary Fund actually benefit multinational corporations, according to Parenti?

There is a "mystery" we must explain: How is it that as corporate investments and foreign aid and international loans to poor countries have increased dramatically throughout the world over the last half century, so has poverty? The number of people living in poverty is growing at a faster rate than the world's population. What do we make of this?

Over the last half century, U.S. industries and banks (and other Western corporations) have invested heavily in those poorer regions of Asia, Africa, and Latin America known as the "Third World." The transnationals are attracted by the rich natural resources, the high return that comes from low-paid labor, and the nearly complete absence of taxes, environmental regulations, worker benefits, and occupational safety costs.

The U.S. government has subsidized this flight of capital by granting corporations tax concessions on their overseas investments, and even paying some of their relocation expenses—much to the outrage of labor unions here at home who see their jobs evaporating.

The transnationals push out local businesses in the Third World and preempt their markets. American agribusiness cartels, heavily subsidized by U.S. taxpayers, dump surplus products in other countries at below cost and undersell local farmers. As Christopher Cook describes it in his *Diet for a Dead Planet*, they expropriate the best land in these countries for cash-crop exports, usually monoculture crops requiring large amounts of pesticides, leaving less and less acreage for the hundreds of varieties of organically grown foods that feed the local populations.

Corporations Exploit the Third World

By displacing local populations from their lands and robbing them of their self-sufficiency, corporations create overcrowded labor markets of desperate people who are forced into shanty towns to toil for poverty wages (when they can get work), often in violation of the countries' own minimum wage laws.

In Haiti, for instance, workers are paid 11 cents an hour by corporate giants such as Disney, Wal-Mart, and J.C. Penney. The United States is one of the few countries that has refused to sign an international convention for the abolition of child labor and forced labor. This position stems from the child labor practices of U.S. corporations throughout the Third World and within the United States itself, where children as young as 12 suffer high rates of injuries and fatalities, and are often paid less than the minimum wage.

The savings that big business reaps from cheap labor abroad are not passed on in lower prices to their customers elsewhere. Corporations do not outsource to far-off regions so that U.S. consumers can save money. They outsource in order to increase their margin of profit. In 1990, shoes made by Indonesian children working twelve-hour days for 13 cents an hour, cost only $2.60 but still sold for $100 or more in the United States.

U.S. foreign aid usually works hand in hand with transnational investment. It subsidizes construction of the infrastructure needed by corporations in the Third World: ports, highways, and refineries.

The aid given to Third World governments comes with strings attached. It often must be spent on U.S. products, and the recipient nation is required to give investment preferences to U.S. companies, shifting consumption away from home produced commodities and foods in favor of imported ones, creating more dependency, hunger, and debt.

A good chunk of the aid money never sees the light of day, going directly into the personal coffers of sticky-fingered officials in the recipient countries.

Poor Nations Forced into Debt

Aid (of a sort) also comes from other sources. In 1944, the United Nations created the World Bank and the International Monetary Fund (IMF). Voting power in both organizations is determined by a country's financial contribution. As the largest "donor," the United States has a dominant voice, followed by Germany, Japan, France, and Great Britain. The IMF operates in secrecy with a select group of bankers and finance ministry staffs drawn mostly from the rich nations.

The World Bank and IMF are supposed to assist nations in their development. What actually happens is another story. A poor country borrows from the World Bank to build up some aspect of its economy. Should it be unable to pay back the heavy interest because of declining export sales or some other reason, it must borrow again, this time from the IMF.

But the IMF imposes a "structural adjustment program" (SAP), requiring debtor countries to grant tax breaks to the transnational corporations, reduce wages, and make no attempt to protect local enterprises from foreign imports and foreign takeovers. The debtor nations are pressured to privatize their economies, selling at scandalously low prices their state-owned mines, railroads, and utilities to private corporations.

They are forced to open their forests to clear-cutting and their lands to strip mining, without regard to the ecological damage done. The debtor nations also must cut back on subsidies for health, education, transportation and food, spending less on their people in order to have more money to meet

Microloans Do Not Alleviate Poverty

Although microcredit yields some noneconomic benefits, it does not significantly alleviate poverty. Indeed, in some instances microcredit makes life at the bottom of the pyramid worse. Contrary to the hype about microcredit, the best way to eradicate poverty is to create jobs and to increase worker productivity.

To understand why creating jobs, not offering microcredit, is the better solution to alleviating poverty, consider these two alternative scenarios: (1) A microfinancier lends $200 to each of 500 women so that each can buy a sewing machine and set up her own sewing microenterprise, or (2) a traditional financier lends $100,000 to one savvy entrepreneur and helps her set up a garment manufacturing business that employs 500 people. In the first case, the women must make enough money to pay off their usually high-interest loans while competing with each other in exactly the same market niche. Meanwhile the garment manufacturing business can exploit economies of scale and use modern manufacturing processes and organizational techniques to enrich not only its owners, but also its workers. . . .

Microloans sometimes even reduce cash flow to the poorest of the poor, observes Vijay Mahajan, the chief executive of Basix, an Indian rural finance institution. He concludes that microcredit "seems to do more harm than good to the poorest." One reason could be the high interest rates charged by microcredit organizations. Acleda, a Cambodian commercial bank specializing in microcredit, charges interest rates of about 2 percent to 4.5 percent each month. Some other microlenders charge more, pushing most annual rates to between 30 percent and 60 percent. Microcredit proponents argue that these rates, although high, are still well below those charged by informal moneylenders. But if poor clients cannot earn a greater return on their investment than the interest they must pay, they will become poorer as a result of microcredit, not wealthier.

Aneel Karnani, Stanford Social Innovation Review,
Summer 2007.

debt payments. Required to grow cash crops for export earnings, they become even less able to feed their own populations.

So it is that throughout the Third World, real wages have declined, and national debts have soared to the point where debt payments absorb almost all of the poorer countries' export earnings—which creates further impoverishment as it leaves the debtor country even less able to provide the things its population needs.

No Trickle Down

Here then we have explained a "mystery." It is, of course, no mystery at all if you don't adhere to trickle-down mystification. Why has poverty deepened while foreign aid and loans and investments have grown? Answer: Loans, investments, and most forms of aid are designed not to fight poverty but to augment the wealth of transnational investors at the expense of local populations.

There is no trickle down, only a siphoning up from the toiling many to the moneyed few.

In their perpetual confusion, some liberal critics conclude that foreign aid and IMF and World Bank structural adjustments "do not work"; the end result is less self-sufficiency and more poverty for the recipient nations, they point out. Why then do the rich member states continue to fund the IMF and World Bank? Are their leaders just less intelligent than the critics who keep pointing out to them that their policies are having the opposite effect?

No, it is the critics who are stupid, not the Western leaders and investors who own so much of the world and enjoy such immense wealth and success. They pursue their aid and foreign loan programs because such programs do work. The question is, work for whom? Cui bono [for whose good]?

The purpose behind their investments, loans, and aid programs is not to uplift the masses in other countries. That is certainly not the business they are in. The purpose is to serve the interests of global capital accumulation, to take over the lands and local economies of Third World peoples, monopolize their markets, depress their wages, indenture their labor with enormous debts, privatize their public service sector, and prevent these nations from emerging as trade competitors by not allowing them a normal development.

In these respects, investments, foreign loans, and structural adjustments work very well indeed.

The real mystery is: why do some people find such an analysis to be so improbable, a "conspiratorial" imagining? Why are they skeptical that U.S. rulers knowingly and deliberately pursue such ruthless policies (suppress wages, rollback environmental protections, eliminate the public sector, cut human services) in the Third World? These rulers are pursuing much the same policies right here in our own country!

Isn't it time that liberal critics stop thinking that the people who own so much of the world—and want to own it all—are "incompetent" or "misguided" or "failing to see the unintended consequences of their policies?" You are not being very smart when you think your enemies are not as smart as you. They know where their interests lie, and so should we.

| "International remittances reduce the level and depth of poverty."

Immigrant Remittances Reduce Poverty in Poor Home Countries

Manuel Orozco et al.

Manuel Orozco is executive director of the Remittances and Rural Development project at Inter-American Dialogue, funded by the Inter-American Development Bank and the UN International Fund for Agricultural Development. In the following viewpoint, Orozco and development researchers Richard H. Adams Jr. of the World Bank; Ernesto Cordova of the Interamerican Development Bank; Rodolfo Zamora of the University of Zacatecas, Mexico; and Sarah J. Mahler of the Centre for Transnational and Comparative Studies at Florida International University examine the multiple benefits of immigrant remittances in reducing global poverty, especially in countries located close to labor-receiving areas, such as Mexico and northern Africa. Poor people spend remittances not only on food, clothing, and shelter, the authors maintain, but also on medical care, education, and sustainable business ventures, so barriers to immigration and the easy flow of remittances across borders should be lowered.

As you read, consider the following questions:

1. On average, how much money do migrant workers send home per year, according to Orozco?

2. What evidence do the authors present to support the assertion that children in remittance-receiving households stay in school longer and get better health care?

3. How do poor women and poor men spend remittances differently, according to the authors?

A t least US$232 billion [was] sent back home globally by around 200 million migrants to their families in 2005, three times official development aid (US$78.6 billion dollars). Moreover, migration and remittance experts argue that the unofficial transfers could be as large as formal flows. What impact is this having on poverty reduction?

Remittances are a portion of the earnings a migrant sends to relatives back home. Most migrant workers send home between US$2,000 and US$5,000 a year—or 20 to 30 percent of their earnings. In most cases, these migrants receive low incomes working in the service or agricultural industry, for example as caterers, cleaners, or farmers. They respond to a demand for foreign labour in the host country.

How Remittances Work

The social and productive base (such as natural resources, human resources and industry) of an economy defines the ways in which remittances function. They should be seen as foreign savings: as with aid, international trade or investment, remittances interact with the structure of the local economy in the home country. . . .

If an economy is unable to produce competitively, its labour force will be reduced and eventually some workers will migrate to take care of their families. But recipient families can only do so much with the money received; they are dependent upon whether their local economy can provide an effective supply of services and products in response to demand.

Consumers' knowledge of what they can get depends on efficient information of the marketplace and a supply-driven economy and business that reacts to remittance recipients' interests (such as savings, credit, education and health). Women, for example, can improve their social position when the local economy offers incentives: if the local economy cannot meet that demand, goods will be imported. . . .

The Challenge for Practitioners

Practitioners (such as donors, national governments, non-governmental organisations) need to create opportunities for remittances to improve and be absorbed into a local economy. Policies must allow remittances to promote development and alleviate the failures or weaknesses of the local economy.

Institutions working on economic development need to focus on three areas:

- *Integrating remittances into the economy of a country*: exploring the interaction between the local productive base of an economy and the cause and effect of remittance and other migrant transfers.

- *The macroeconomic behaviour of remittances*: specifically, that of the factors that generally influence responses of productive forces such as investment or trade. This means paying close attention to the effect that price increases, foreign exchange rate fluctuations, interest rates or unemployment have on sending remittances home.

- *The impact of remittances on economic growth*: this is particularly important in countries with a strong impact on national income, particularly where remittances represent more than 5 percent of a country's Gross Domestic Product, or 30 percent of total exports.

Policy Implications

The following policy options would strengthen 'transnational' families and the home country's economy:

Reduce transaction costs. The average cost of sending money home is almost 10 percent of the total sent, due to market inefficiencies such as lack of competition, use of costly transfer methods and inadequate means of transferring money. Policies need to encourage a competitive environment, adopt and promote cost-effective and value-added payment technologies attractive to consumers.

Develop financial democracy. Making use of remittances to assist in providing access to financial systems and affordable financial services is an important policy tool. Senders and recipients need access to bank accounts, savings, loans, insurance services and so on; commercial and microfinance institutions can attract senders and recipients into the financial system and increase savings. They can also use remittances within the community for entrepreneurial activities. Offering women access to financial institutions is particularly important as they are often excluded from credit and savings opportunities.

Improve health and education. At least 10 percent of remittances are spent on education and health. Insurance and banking institutions can work with schools and health care systems to offer services such as health insurance and scholarship investment funds. Governments and the private sector can promote investment in education funds to increase enrolment rates, school attendance and length of time spent in education for children in communities receiving remittances.

Promote tourism and trade. One third of migrant remittance senders visit their home country once a year and spend an average of US$1,000 per stay, buying home-produced goods. This demand for tourism and trade is often unmet [because of] an inadequate supply of services and goods. Governments and private sector institutions need to develop profit-making schemes such as investing in small hotels and introducing migrants to lesser-known tourist attractions in their home countries.

State policy for migrants abroad. The huge number of migrants worldwide and their engagement with the home country means that governments need to promote an outreach policy to the community living abroad. This would build confidence between the diaspora [those living away from their home country] and the state, enhance and strength links between the two and ensure joint development strategies.

Do no harm. Remittances are first and foremost a private family affair: no one can tell other people what to do with their money. Taxation or imposing tough measures is harmful to individuals already facing serious constraints. Regulatory measures that are harmful to senders will reduce the impact remittances have on development. . . .

Do Remittances Reduce Poverty?

What is the impact of international remittances on the level of poverty (the share of the population living below the poverty line) and the depth of poverty (how far the income of the average poor person is below the poverty line)? How do remittances from abroad enable households to escape from poverty in large labour-exporting countries such as Mexico, Guatemala, the Philippines and Ghana?

New research by the World Bank's International Migration and Development Research Programme shows that:

- International remittances reduce the level and depth of poverty. For example, a 10 percent increase in international remittances from each individual migrant will lead to a 3.5 percent decline in the share of people living in poverty.

- While remittances reduce poverty, countries with higher levels of poverty are not necessarily receiving more remittances. Countries with the highest levels of poverty—such as those in sub-Saharan Africa—do not produce many international migrants and therefore receive fewer remittances.

- In general, the largest effects of remittances on poverty are observed in countries located close to major labour-receiving areas. Developing countries close to the United States or Europe tend to receive more remittances which are usually spread evenly among the population. In Guatemala, for example, international remittances reduce the level of poverty by 1.6 percent and the depth of poverty by 12.6 percent; remittances account for over 60 percent of household income for the poorest 10 percent of the population.

It is sometimes thought that international remittances go mainly to rich people and that therefore remittances will tend to increase income inequality in developing countries. However, the World Bank research finds that international remittances have little impact on income inequality. For instance, in Guatemala and Ghana, including remittances in household income leads to only a slight increase in income inequality. This means that most of the positive impacts of remittances on poverty come from increases in household income, rather than any changes in the level of income distribution in a country....

Improving Health and Education

The Inter-American Development Bank (IADB) estimates remittance flows to Latin American and Caribbean countries at over US$45 billion in 2004. In 2005 they will have reached US$55 billion—higher than foreign direct investment and overseas development assistance to the region. The magnitude of such transfers raises important questions about their development impact and how national governments and the international community can maximise their potential.

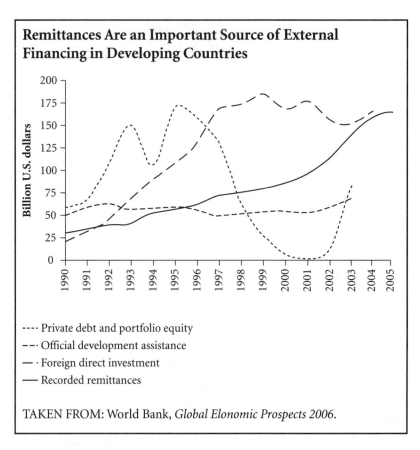

Remittances Are an Important Source of External Financing in Developing Countries

---- Private debt and portfolio equity
–– Official development assistance
— · Foreign direct investment
— Recorded remittances

TAKEN FROM: World Bank, *Global Elonomic Prospects 2006.*

Remittances may improve education and health as they allow families to supplement their limited incomes and invest in the future. Examining the impact of remittances separately from other effects of migration is difficult, however. The possibility of emigrating, and remittance income itself, may affect people's work and schooling decisions. Migration may disrupt family life and influence children's performance at school. Migrants may get better information about health care that they then share with their families back home.

An increasing number of studies show that the overall effect of remittances on education and health is positive.

Evidence indicates that children from recipient households stay in school longer:

- In El Salvador, US$100 of remittance income lowers the probability of children leaving school by 54 percent in urban areas.

- In the Philippines, a 10 percent rise in household income through remittances leads to a proportional increase in enrolment rates among children aged 17 to 21.

- Across Mexican rural municipalities, illiteracy among children aged 6 to 14 falls by three percent when the number of households receiving remittances rises by one percent.

Remittances play an important role if the public health care system is unable to provide universal health insurance or adequate treatment and preventative care. Studies in Mexico show that:

- An additional *peso* in remittance transfers raises households' health care expenditure by between 6 and 9 *centavos*.

- Infant mortality falls and birth weight among Mexican children improves with remittances. A one percent rise in the portion of households receiving remittances reduces by 1.2 lives the number of children who die in their first year.

- Remittances may reduce infant mortality by improving housing conditions, allowing mothers to stay home and care for the newborn baby, or by improving access to public services such as drinking water.

What can the international community and national governments do to strengthen the developmental impact of remittances? The IADB and other institutions recommend:

- lowering the cost of sending remittances home by increasing competition among service providers, improving payment system infrastructure and removing regulatory barriers

- promoting financial democracy by encouraging greater use of the banking system

- promoting greater remittance flows by avoiding taxation and overregulation

- enhancing their local development impact by supporting hometown associations (groups of migrants from the same community)

- improving housing conditions by offering mortgage loans to migrants

- encouraging banks to offer new financial products to migrant families, such as health insurance policies

- working with hometown associations to improve education and health infrastructure

A consensus is emerging among international organisations and national governments to work in these areas. Facilitating remittance flows should allow recipient families worldwide to offer their children a brighter future. . . .

Latin American Successes

More than 30 million Latin American migrants live and work abroad. Approximately 18 million live in the USA; 16 million send between US$200 and US$300 back to their families every month.

The Inter-American Development Bank (IADB) estimates that Latin American and Caribbean migrants sent home US$45.8 billion in 2004, making Latin America and the Caribbean one of the highest remittance-receiving regions in the world. Mexico alone received US$16.6 billion in 2004—more than any other country in the world and a 25 percent increase from 2003. The second largest amounts received in the region were by Brazil (US$5.6 billion) and Colombia (US$3.9 billion).

IADB research shows that remittances have an enormous potential to contribute to poverty reduction and economic development if invested in infrastructure and employment activities, for example, in migrants' home communities.

Research findings include:

- In Central America approximately 90 percent of remittances are spent on basic family needs, including education and healthcare. The remaining 10 percent is saved or invested.

- Households receiving remittances tend to have better nutrition and access to health and educational services compared to households that do not. Remittances improve the wellbeing of those who receive them; they also create a form of social hierarchy between those who receive and those who do not.

- The poorest regions of Mexico are not the main regions sending migrants or receiving remittances.

Zacatecas is a state with over 100 years history of migration to the USA and the highest percentage of its residents living abroad of any Mexican state. For over 15 years Zacatecan migrants have been using remittances to finance social infrastructure projects back home, such as drinking water systems, school renovations, electrification and road construction. From 1993 to 2004, Zacatecan hometown associations (groups of migrants from the same community) spent over US$164.8 million from remittances on 1,500 community projects; the Mexican government matched these investments with approximately US$483 million. . . .

Gender Matters

Most studies examine how much money is sent home, how to lower transfer costs or what percentage of a country's Gross Domestic Product remittances represent. Remittances reflect and transmit power yet very little research exists on the gender issues involved.

The few studies that do exist offer some provocative findings. Survey data from senders and receivers of both sexes report that remittances are spent on basic family welfare such as food, clothing and education. However, in Latin American and the Caribbean slightly more women than men report using remittances for investments, savings and businesses.

Observational data from fieldwork offer additional insights:

- Women spend most of their remittances on their families' basic needs while men spend more on non-necessities.

- While a common household economy is often assumed, spouses frequently send remittances independently and for different purposes.

- Government officials in highly patriarchal societies such as Mexico often exclude female migrants from decision-making roles regarding how collective remittances should be invested in local development projects.

- Remittances increasingly finance poor countries that discriminate against females. The Filipino government used to require female domestic workers to remit 50 percent of their earnings. Today these workers are disproportionately blamed for family disintegration while their non-migrant husbands, who often squander remittances, are portrayed as sacrificing for their families.

- When female migrants send remittances home they improve their social standing in their families. This is important especially when they are excluded from 'traditional' means of increasing status enjoyed only by males. For example, in Thailand only sons may join religious orders or perform ancestral rites.

- Receiving remittances—particularly in the absence of other income—increases recipients' dependency upon remitters. However, in countries where males usually control household income, female recipients in particular become empowered as they control how remittances are spent. In rural El Salvador and elsewhere negotiations between remitting and recipient husbands and wives are a major strain on relationships and families in general.

  Gender is often mistakenly seen as a synonym for women, when it should refer to the social forces that determine acceptable male/female behaviour and how men and women relate to each other. The research findings show that a truly gender-based approach to remittances is urgently needed.

- Governments and international organisations should commission studies that incorporate gender into their design and analysis and include work on how senders and recipients interact with financial institutions.

- Research should include surveys and direct observation.

- Research results must be widely disseminated particularly to policymakers who should incorporate them in planning and implementation.

- Female and male migrants and recipients should be involved in policy and decision-making.

- Gender policies must address men as well as women, a shift that is likely to motivate male policymakers to take gender more seriously.

> "Can remittances solve the problem of poverty globally? Despite the hype, the answer is no."

Immigrant Workers' Remittances Cannot Solve Global Poverty

Elizabeth Boyle

Elizabeth Boyle is an associate professor of sociology and law at the University of Minnesota in Minneapolis. In the following viewpoint, Boyle uses the example of her own immigrant Italian grandfather to argue that remittances to poor home countries cannot resolve global poverty today any more than they could a century ago. The relief remittances offer, Boyle maintains, is temporary, uneven, and in the long term, too costly to poor countries.

As you read, consider the following questions:

1. How does the author's own experience support her argument that remittances are beneficial only in the short term?

Elizabeth Boyle, "Migrants Solving Global Poverty? A Nice Idea But. . . ," *Contemporary Perspectives on Immigration*, March 2, 2007. Reproduced by permission of the author.

2. How does Boyle show that most migrants' money goes to the wealthiest countries?

3. How does emigration from poorer countries actually harm the poor there, in Boyle's view?

When my Grandfather Cianciaruso was a young man, he worked as a shoe repairman in Iowa, and every month he sent most of the money he earned back to his mother in Italy. At that time, it was common for migrants to send money back to family members (these payments are called "remittances"). And remittances are still exceedingly common among new migrants today. The more things stay the same, the more things change, however. Today, remittances are viewed as a possible solution to global inequality and poverty. From where does this view come, and how realistic is it?

Overly Optimistic Messages

The international financial system, including the World Bank, is the source of this new vision of remittances. International investors believe they can harness remittances to provide security for loans to poor countries. Better security means lower interest rates for borrowing countries and more steady interest payments for lenders/investors. Remittances may also provide basic services that governments are unable to afford in poor countries. What seems to get lost in these discussions is that migrants' financial support of their families is not a new source of income. The pie can be cut into new shapes and slices, but in the end the size of the pie does not increase (unless migration increases, a point I will return to below).

The overly optimistic message about remittances has been getting lots of attention recently, as newspapers have been filled with remittance success stories. The *New York Times*, using Inter-American Development Bank statistics, reported that remittances are the "largest and most direct poverty reduction program" in Latin America, greatly exceeding the amount of

Remittances Mask Governments' Failures

Millions of unemployed Mexicans are now dependent upon money wired from the United States, where low-skill wages are now nine times higher than in Mexico. On the national level, such subsidies, like oil windfall profits, allow just enough money to hide the government's failure to promote the proper economic conditions—through the protection of property rights, tax reform, transparent investment laws, modern infrastructure, etc.—that would eventually lead to decent housing and well-paying jobs.

It may be counterintuitive to think that checks from hard-working expatriates are pernicious. But for a developing nation, remittances can prove as problematic as the proverbial plight of the lottery winner—sudden winnings that were not earned. In short, remittances, along with oil and tourism—not agriculture, engineering, education, manufacturing or finance—prop up an otherwise ailing Mexican economy. This helps explain why half of the country's 106 million citizens still live in poverty.

Victor Davis Hanson,
Real Clear Politics, *May 11, 2006.*

foreign aid doled out by the United States to countries in that region. Celia Dugger reported in another *Times* article that remittances were a factor in reducing poverty in Nepal from 42 percent of the population to only (?) 31 percent. Meanwhile, the South Florida *Sun-Sentinel* covered the story of Guatemala President Oscar Berger Perdamo's visit to Jupiter, Florida. During a meeting with Guatemalan expatriates, the President exclaimed, "Thanks for those blessed remittances. They have allowed your families to rise from poverty." There is no doubt that remittances are important. For families that receive them, they can even make the difference between life and death.

Realistic Shortcomings

But can remittances solve the problem of poverty globally? Despite the hype, the answer is no. First, consider that while Grandpa Cianciaruso regularly sent money to Italy, neither I nor any of his other grandchildren picked up that burden. Remittances are common for first-generation immigrants, but become very rare by the third generation. Unless they are continuous and replenished, remittances will only be beneficial to the poor in the short term. Consider that remittances have been around for a long time—and so has global poverty.

The second reason that remittances cannot solve global inequality is that they tend to track existing wealth patterns rather than change them. To better understand the flow of remittances, the World Bank divided countries into four groups based on their GDP [gross domestic product] in 2005—high-income, upper-middle income, lower-middle income, and low-income.

The organization found that the remittances going to individuals in the high-income group of countries ($125.3 billion) dwarfed the remittances going to individuals in all of the other groups combined ($24.1 billion). The top five national recipients of remittances in 2004 were India, China, Mexico, France, and the Philippines—not the poorest countries in the world by a long shot. When remittances are measured as a percentage of GDP rather than in raw numbers, more poor countries are among the top recipients (such as Haiti). Nevertheless, the fact remains that most migrants' money goes to the wealthiest countries. The World Bank's own report on remittances to Latin America concludes that remittances are "neither 'manna from heaven' nor a substitute for sound development policies."

Yet another problem is the unhealthy incentives that chasing remittances place on national governments in poorer countries. The lure of remittances from former residents prompts countries to encourage emigration. The *Stabroek News*[in Guyana] reports that the "most common Caribbean export is not sugar, rice, coffee, bananas, bauxite, but its people." In the Nepali case "success story" above, remittances came at a high price. Remittances quadrupled from 1996 to 2004, but by the end of that period, 1 out of every 11 adult Nepali men was working abroad. The outward flow of a country's most talented citizens will hurt that country in the long run. Encouraging emigration to enhance remittances also tends to undermine cooperation between countries, such as the U.S. and Mexico, to limit undocumented migration. Thus, chasing remittances leads to some troubling policy outcomes. It may be helpful in the short term, but it takes a serious toll in the long term.

No Cure for Poverty

Sending money to less fortunate loved-ones is a wonderful, generous act. It illustrates what many of us see every day—that migrants have a strong work ethic and are deeply devoted to their families. Remittances offer desperately-needed relief and special opportunities to many individuals in poor countries. Despite their benefits, however, remittances are not a cure for global poverty. They did not lead to greater economic equality a century ago; they will not do so today. And the cost of formally encouraging remittances has a high price tag; a cost that will have to be paid by poor countries eventually.

Periodical Bibliography

The following articles have been selected to supplement the diverse views presented in this chapter.

Francis Calpotura   "Remittances: For Love and Money," *Foreign Policy in Focus*, August 14, 2007.

Raj M. Desai   "The Political Economy of Poverty Reduction," Brookings Institution, November 2007. www.brookings.edu/papers/2007/11_pov erty_desai.aspx?more=rc.

Garry Emmons   "The Business of Global Poverty," *Working Knowledge*, April 4, 2007. http://hbswk.hbs.edu/item/5656.html.

International Monetary Fund   "Debt Relief Under the Heavily Indebted Poor Countries (HIPC) Initiative," factsheet, October 2007. www.imf.org/external/np/exr/facts/hipc.htm.

Craig Leisher, Pieter van Beukering, and Lea M. Scherl   "Nature's Investment Bank: How Marine Protected Areas Contribute to Poverty Reduction," *Nature Conservancy*, December 2007.

Matthew Quirk   "Bright Lights, Big Cities," *Atlantic Monthly*, December 2007.

Martin Ravallion   "Urban Poverty: Are Poor People Gravitating to Towns and Cities? Yes, But Maybe Not Quickly Enough," *Finance & Development*, September 2007.

Robert J. Samuelson   "The Global Poverty Trap," *Newsweek*, October 31, 2007.

World Bank   "Global Economic Prospects 2008: Technology Diffusion in the Developing World," annual flagship report, January 2008. http://siteresour ces.worldbank.org/INTGEP2008/Resources/GEP _complete.pdf.

For Further Discussion

Chapter 1

1. John Cassidy says the Census Bureau's official poverty measures have numerous shortcomings. How would the overall poverty rate change if it were based on any of the following alternative measures: after-tax income, income that includes the value of noncash benefits such as food stamps and Medicaid, consideration of family members' different needs and expenses based on age and family size?

2. Robert Rector defines poverty largely on the basis of material possessions, Michelle Conlin and Aaron Bernstein on the basis of wage rates, and Tony Pugh on demographic factors. Using evidence from the viewpoints, which author makes the most valid argument? How do you think poverty should be defined?

3. Arloc Sherman and Aviva Aron-Dine identify a widening gap between rich and poor in America. Alan Reynolds uses the same reported-income data to argue that the income difference between the richest and poorest Americans is not growing. How do these authors use the same evidence to draw different conclusions?

Chapter 2

1. Robert Rector argues that low-skill immigration increases poverty and should be strictly limited. Jeff Chapman and Jared Bernstein contend that the contributions of high-skill immigrants have produced a net fiscal gain, and that immigration is not the cause of rising poverty rates. Which argument do you find more persuasive, and why?

2. Alan Jenkins is the director of a social justice advocacy organization concerned with racial equality and labor rights. Blake Bailey is affiliated with a conservative think tank that opposes expansion of federal welfare programs. John Peterson is the editor of a socialist, pro-labor union journal. How might these authors' professional positions affect their objectivity on the issue of the causes of poverty? Do you detect any evidence of bias in their viewpoints? Explain your answer.

3. Robert Rector, Alan Jenkins, and John Peterson all advance generic theories of poverty—that is, cite contributing factors that are largely beyond individual control. On what grounds do these authors disagree, and on what grounds do they agree? In your view, are generic theories of poverty more or less persuasive than individual theories such as that advanced by Blake Bailey? Why?

Chapter 3

1. Compare the advantages of raising the minimum wage presented by Jason Furman and Sharon Parrot with the disadvantages of raising the minimum wage presented by David Henderson. Is a higher minimum wage justified, in your view? Why or why not?

2. John Podesta argues that a package of government programs and tax breaks will significantly cut the poverty rate. Ron Haskins and Isabel Sawhill argue that the poverty rate fell in the 1990s because government benefits were cut during this period. Use examples from the viewpoints to distinguish between correlations and true cause-and-effect relationships. Based on your findings, which author makes the more persuasive argument?

3. Matthew Ladner believes tax cuts help the poor, while the National Organization for Women believes that tax cuts hurt the poor. Are these claims mutually exclusive? If yes, why? If not, how might both claims be true?

4. Clive Crook calls Charles Murray's proposal to scrap existing benefit programs and pay all Americans ten thousand dollars a year for life an outlandish and unworkable plan but suggests no new alternative. Based on the viewpoints in this chapter, how effective are existing antipoverty policies, and what possibly radical new ideas can you suggest for consideration?

Chapter 4

1. In what ways might climate change affect both World Bank projections of Millennium Project progress in reducing global poverty and Conn Hallinan's criticism of the Millennium Project goals?

2. George C. Lodge and Craig Wilson argue that economic growth is the way out of poverty and multinational corporations (MNCs) know best how to achieve this. Michael Parenti portrays MNCs as a cause of global poverty and World Bank programs ostensibly designed as a way for developing countries to raise their citizens' standard of living as primarily beneficial to corporate interests. Based on your reading of the viewpoints, what role should government play in reducing global poverty, and to what extent should private enterprise assume that responsibility?

3. Worldwide, migrants send an estimated $300 billion per year to relatives in home countries. Manuel Orozco and his coauthors portrays these remittances as a vital tool in reducing global poverty, but Elizabeth Boyle views remittances as short-term relief at best. How do these arguments affect your view of immigration policy and of the reliance of cash-strapped governments on remittances as an antipoverty strategy?

Organizations to Contact

The editors have compiled the following list of organizations concerned with the issues debated in this book. The descriptions are derived from materials provided by the organizations. All have publications or information available for interested readers. The list was compiled on the date of publication of the present volume; street and online addresses may change. Be aware that many organizations take several weeks or longer to respond to inquiries, so allow as much time as possible.

American Enterprise Institute (AEI)
1150 Seventeenth St. NW, Washington, DC   20036
(202) 862-5800 • fax: (202) 862-7177
Web site: www.aei.org

The American Enterprise Institute for Public Policy Research is an independent, nonprofit research organization associated with the neoconservative movement in American foreign policy and Republican administrations since the 1980s. AEI scholars advocate limited government, tax reduction, capitalist enterprise, and individual responsibility as the best responses to poverty. The AEI Web site offers an archive of op-eds, newsletters, position papers, government testimony, and longer monographs on poverty-related topics such as welfare and health insurance reform, as well as the daily online business magazine the *American*.

America's Second Harvest
35 E. Wacker Dr., #2000, Chicago, IL   60601
(800) 771-2303 • fax: (202) 546-7005
Web site: www.secondharvest.org

The nation's largest charitable hunger-relief organization, America's Second Harvest is a network of more than two hundred member food banks and food-rescue groups that supply food pantries, soup kitchens, emergency shelters, and after-school programs across the country. The network provides food assistance to an estimated 25 million low-income hungry people each year. The organization publishes *Hunger in America 2006*, a profile of the incidence of hunger and food insecurity in the United States. Its Web site explains the network's history and operations, provides a local food-bank locator, and encourages citizen participation in useful sections called Who We Help, Who Helps Us, How We Work, and How to Help.

Brookings Institution
1775 Massachusetts Ave. NW, Washington, DC   20036
(202) 797-6000 • fax: (202) 797-6004
e-mail: brookinfo@brook.edu
Web site: www.brookings.org

The institution, founded in 1927, is a liberal-centrist think tank whose fellows conduct research on and debate issues of foreign policy, economics, government, and the social sciences. Its scholars publish analyses of domestic and global antipoverty policy in the quarterly journal *Brookings Review* and in position papers such as "Attacking Poverty and Inequality" (2008), which recommends strengthening work requirements for government assistance; raising the minimum wage; expanding the earned income tax credit; subsidizing child care for low-wage workers; and funding early childhood education, family planning, and teen pregnancy prevention programs.

Cato Institute
1000 Massachusetts Ave. NW, Washington, DC   20001
(202) 842-0200 • fax: (202) 842-3490
e-mail: cato@cato.org
Web site: www.cato.org

The institute is a libertarian public policy research foundation dedicated to individual liberty, free markets, and limited government. It opposes, for example, minimum wage laws, trade barriers, and expansion of executive power; it supports noninterventionist foreign policy, a balanced federal budget, and workers' right to opt out of the Social Security program. It offers numerous publications on public policy, including the triannual *Cato Journal*, the bimonthly newsletter *Cato Policy Report*, and the quarterly magazine *Regulation*. Numerous poverty-related studies and position papers are available on its Web site, categorized under useful headings such as "Health, Welfare, and Entitlements," "Immigration and Labor Markets," and "International Economics and Development."

Center on Budget and Policy Priorities (CBPP)
820 First St. NE, Suite 510, Washington, DC   20002
(202) 408-1080 • fax: (202) 408-1056
e-mail: center@cbpp.org
Web site: www.cbpp.org

The center is a nonprofit research and advocacy group that researches and represents the needs of low-income people in setting budget and tax policy. Founded in 1981 to analyze federal budget priorities, the center expanded its focus in the 1990s to funding for the poor at the state level (the State Fiscal Analysis Initiative) and in developing countries (the International Budget Project). The CBPP maintains an online library of reports, statistics, slide shows, and same-day analyses of the government's poverty and income data.

Children's Defense Fund (CDF)
25 E St. NW, Washington, DC   20001
(800-233-1200)
e-mail: cdfinfo@childrensdefense.org
Web site: www.childrensdefense.org

The CDF, founded in 1973, is a private, nonprofit organization whose self-described mission is to ensure the health, education, and safety of all children. Led by founder and president Marian Wright Edelman, the fund lobbies legislators in support of Medicaid and the Children's Health Insurance Program (CHIP), the Head Start early education program, and other services for disadvantaged and poor children. Numerous publications are available for free download from the fund's Web site, including *America's Cradle to Prison Pipeline* and *The State of America's Children.*

Economic Policy Institute (EPI)
1333 H St. NW, Suite 300, East Tower
Washington, DC 20005-4707
(202) 775-8810 • fax: (202) 775-0819
e-mail: researchdept@epi.org
Web site: www.epi.org

EPI is a nonprofit, progressive think tank created in 1986 to represent the interests of low- and middle-income workers in the debate over U.S. economic policy. It supports minimum-wage laws and workers' right to form unions. Its fellows track trends in wages, benefits, union participation, and other economic indicators; testify before Congress and state legislatures; advise policy makers; and publish books, studies, and issue guides on poverty-related topics such as welfare, offshoring, and the living wage. EPI also produces the biennial *The State of Working America* and the 2007 briefing paper "Economy's Gains Fail to Reach Most Workers' Paychecks."

GovBenefits.gov
(800) 333-4636
Web site: www.govbenefits.gov

Sponsored by a partnership of federal agencies including all cabinet-level departments, the Social Security Administration, and the U.S. Small Business Administration, GovBenefits.gov is the official benefits Web site of the U.S. government, with the most comprehensive and up-to-date information on more than 1,000 federal and state benefits and assistance programs for poor Americans. Easily navigable (and searchable by state), the site explains eligibility requirements and provides links for food/nutrition (such as food stamps and WIC), education, housing, health care, and job-training programs. It is a valuable resource for classroom discussion of welfare reform and the effectiveness of existing antipoverty programs, as well as comparisons of antipoverty initiatives in different states.

Grameen Bank
Mirpur-1, Dhaka   1216
  Bangladesh
(88 02) 9005257-69
e-mail: g_trust@grameen.com
Web site: www.grameen-info.org

Winner of the 2006 Nobel Peace Prize, the Grameen Bank is an example of the microcredit, or microfinance, approach to reducing global poverty—issuing collateral-free loans averaging one hundred dollars to the poorest of the poor to establish small businesses at the village level. Founded by Bangladeshi economist Muhammad Yunus in 1976, Grameen is 94 percent owned by and works exclusively for its borrowers, 97 percent of whom are women. As of December 2007 the bank had disbursed $6.7 billion. With a loan recovery rate of 98.35 percent, Grameen finances 100 percent of its loans through borrower deposits and accepts no donor money. The bank's quarterly newsletter *Grameen Dialogue* and comprehensive Web site, including FAQs, detailed balance sheets, and explanations of initiatives such as interest-free credit to beggars and housing and education loans, are sources for understanding how microfinance works in the developing world.

The Heritage Foundation
214 Massachusetts Ave. NE, Washington, DC   20002
(202) 546-4400 • fax: (202) 546-0904
e-mail: info@heritage.org
Web site: www.heritage.org

The foundation is a conservative public policy research institute dedicated to "principles of free enterprise, limited government, individual freedom, traditional American values, and a strong national defense." Its resident scholars publish position papers on a wide range of complex issues in its Backgrounder series and much of this material is published in a shorter-length, non-highly-technical, executive summary format that is accessible to student researchers. Numerous poverty-related documents also are archived on the Web site under subject headings such as Welfare, Family and Marriage, Health Care, Entitlements, and Foreign Aid.

Poverty in America: One Nation, Pulling Apart
EMS Environment Institute, Penn State University
University Park, PA   16802-6813
(814) 865-8188
e-mail: akg1@psu.edu
Web site: www.povertyinamerica.psu.edu

This project of Pennsylvania State University's Earth and Environmental Systems Institute professor of geography and regional planning Amy K. Glasmeier describes poor people in America as "people who work or who are dependents of people who work and face limited opportunity, often due to living in places that are seriously disadvantaged because of geography or history or both." The project reports on nationwide social and economic conditions, the history and geography of poverty from 1960 to the present, the effects of welfare reform, and federal expenditures in distressed communities, available online. The Web site also offers several interactive features useful to students, including a living wage calculator, an atlas of poverty in America, and a toolbox for assessing the economic health of a student's own local community.

Progressive Policy Institute (PPI)
600 Pennsylvania Ave. SE, Ste. 400, Washington, DC   20003
(202) 546-0001 • fax: (202) 544-5014
Web site: www.ppionline.org

PPI is a public policy research organization that strives to develop alternatives to what it considers an obsolete left-right debate over poverty. Affiliated with the think tank Democratic Leadership Council's Third Way Foundation, PPI advocates economic policies designed to stimulate broad upward mobility and social policies designed to liberate the poor from poverty and dependence on government support. An extensive library of policy reports is available online, including "Making Work Pay" and "Gimme Shelter," and PPI offers free subscription to e-mail newsletters.

United Nations Development Programme
One United Nations Plaza, New York, NY   10017
(212) 906-6592 • fax: (212) 906-5364
e-mail: mdg.support@undp.org
Web site: www.undp.org

In January 2007 the UN Millennium Project—eight global development goals adopted by 189 nations in 2000—was folded into the United Nations Development Programme, the UN network that helps governments address development problems such as democratic governance, poverty reduction, crisis prevention and recovery, energy and environment use, and HIV/AIDs. The most relevant resources can be found in the site's Millennium Development Goals and Poverty Reduction sections, which explain and track in detail worldwide efforts to achieve Millennium Goal 1 (MDG1), the commitment to cut global poverty in half by 2015.

U.S. Census Bureau Poverty Statistics
4600 Silver Hill Rd., Washington, DC   20233
(301) 763-2422
e-mail: pop@census.gov
Web site: www.census.gov/hhes/www/poverty/poverty.html

The Census Bureau is the official source of statistics on poverty in America. Sections of its Web site cover how poverty is measured; definitions of poverty-related terms; up-to-date dollar amounts used to determine poverty status; FAQs; poverty causes and projections; and comparisons with poverty in foreign countries. Numerous reports and briefs available for download include the annual *Income, Poverty, and Health Insurance Coverage in the United States* and *The Effects of Taxes and Transfers on Income and Poverty in the United States.*

World Bank PovertyNet
1818 H St. NW, Washington, DC   20433
(202) 473-1000 • fax: (202) 477-6391
e-mail: pic@worldbank.org
Web site: http://go.worldbank.org/33CTPSVDC0

PovertyNet is the World Bank's comprehensive source of information on key global poverty issues, measurement, monitoring, analysis, and poverty reduction strategies, including World Bank lending policies. Resources include an e-mail newsletter; reports on the links between poverty and violent conflict, climate change, and immigration; archives of news articles; and country-by-country poverty statistics. The *Global Monitoring Report (GMR) 2007* is available for download in full or summary format.

Bibliography of Books

Rebecca M. Blank
Sheldon H.
Danziger, and
Robert F. Schoeni,
eds.
Working and Poor: How Economic and Policy Changes Are Affecting Low-Wage Workers. New York: Russell Sage Foundation, 2006.

Lael Brainard and
Derek Chollet,
eds.
Too Poor for Peace? Global Poverty, Conflict, and Security in the 21st Century. Washington, DC: Brookings Institution Press, 2007

Fantu Cheru and
Colin Bradford,
eds.
The Millennium Development Goals: Raising the Resources to Tackle World Poverty. London: Zed, 2006.

Glynn Cochrane
Festival Elephants and the Myth of Global Poverty. Boston: Allyn & Bacon, 2008.

Paul Collier
The Bottom Billion: Why the Poorest Countries Are Failing and What Can Be Done About It. New York: Oxford University Press, 2007.

Janet M. Currie
The Invisible Safety Net: Protecting the Nation's Poor Children and Families. Princeton, NJ: Princeton University Press, 2006.

Mike Davis
Planet of Slums. New York: Verso, 2006.

William Easterly
The White Man's Burden: Why the West's Efforts to Aid the Rest Have Done So Much Ill and So Little Good. New York: Penguin, 2006.

Kathryn Edin and
Maria Kefalas
Promises I Can Keep. Berkeley and Los Angeles: University of California Press, 2005.

John Edwards,
Marion Crain,
and Ame L.
Kalleberg, eds.
Ending Poverty in America. New York: New Press, 2007.

Barbara
Ehrenreich
Nickel and Dimed: On (Not) Getting By in America. New York: Holt, 2002.

Jeffrey Grogger
and Lynn A.
Karoly
Welfare Reform: Effects of a Decade of Change. Cambridge, MA: Harvard University Press, 2005.

Heidi Hartmann
Women, Work, and Poverty. Binghamton, NY: Haworth, 2006.

Sharon Hays
Flat Broke with Children. New York: Oxford University Press, 2004.

John Iceland
Poverty in America. 2nd. ed. Berkeley and Los Angeles: University of California Press, 2006.

Charles Karelis
The Persistence of Poverty: Why the Economics of the Well-Off Can't Help the Poor. New Haven, CT: Yale University Press, 2007.

Laura Lein et al.
Life After Welfare: Reform and the Persistence of Poverty. Austin: University of Texas Press, 2007.

Philip Martin,
Michael Fix, and
J. Edward Taylor
The New Rural Poverty: Agriculture and Immigration in California. Washington, DC: Urban Institute Press, 2006.

Charles Murray	*In Our Hands: A Plan to Replace the Welfare State.* Washington, DC: AEI Press, 2006.
Katherine S. Newman and Victor Tan Chen	*The Missing Class: Portraits of the Near Poor in America.* Boston: Beacon, 2007.
Thomas Pogge, ed.	*Freedom from Poverty as a Human Right: Who Owes What to the Very Poor?* New York: Oxford University Press, 2007.
Paul Polak	*Out of Poverty: What Works When Traditional Approaches Fail.* San Francisco: Berrett-Koehler, 2008.
Mark Robert Rank	*One Nation, Underprivileged: Why American Poverty Affects Us All.* New York: Oxford University Press, 2005.
Jeffrey Sachs	*The End of Poverty: Economic Possibilities for Our Time.* New York: Penguin, 2006.
Karen Seccombe	*So You Think I Drive a Cadillac? Welfare Recipients' Perspectives on the System and Its Reform.* Boston: Allyn & Bacon, 2006.
David Shipler	*The Working Poor: Invisible in America.* New York: Vintage, 2005.
Philip Smith and Eric Thurman	*A Billion Bootstraps: Microcredit, Barefoot Banking, and the Business Solution for Ending Poverty.* New York: McGraw-Hill, 2007.

Frank Stricker — *Why America Lost the War on Poverty—and How to Win It.* Chapel Hill: University of North Carolina Press, 2007.

Michael D. Tanner — *The Poverty of Welfare: Helping Others in the Civil Society.* Washington, DC: Cato Institute, 2003.

Louis Uchitelle — *The Disposable American: Layoffs and Their Consequences.* New York: Knopf, 2006.

Sudhir Alladi Venkatesh — *Off the Books: The Underground Economy of the Urban Poor.* Cambridge, MA: Harvard University Press, 2006.

William Vollmann — *Poor People.* New York: Ecco, 2007.

Mark Winne — *Closing the Food Gap: Resetting the Table in the Land of Plenty.* Boston, Beacon, 2008.

Quentin Wodon — *Migration, Remittances, and Poverty.* Washington, DC: World Bank, 2008.

Muhammad Yunus and Karl Weber — *Creating a World Without Poverty.* New York: Perseus, 2007.

Index